3/04

The Syntax of Class

The Syntax of Class

WRITING INEQUALITY
IN NINETEENTH-CENTURY
AMERICA

Amy Schrager Lang

PRINCETON UNIVERSITY PRESS

PRINCETON AND OXFORD

Library of Congress Cataloging-in-Publication Data
Lang, Amy Schrager.
The syntax of class : writing inequality in
nineteenth-century America / Amy Schrager Lang.
p. cm.
Includes bibliographical references and index.
ISBN 0-691-11389-0 (acid-free paper)
1. American fiction—19th century—History and criticism.
2. Social classes in literature. 3. Literature and society—United States—
History—19th century. 4. Social conflict in literature.
5. Sex role in literature. 6. Race in literature. I. Title.
PS374.S68 L36 2003
810.9'355—dc21   2002030780
British Library Cataloging-in-Publication Data is available.

This book has been composed in Sabon typeface.
Printed on acid-free paper. ∞
www.pupress.princeton.edu

Printed in the United States of America
1 3 5 7 9 10 8 6 4 2

Jules Schrager

1917–1980

CONTENTS

ACKNOWLEDGMENTS

SOME BOOKS are waylaid by life, and this is one of them. During the too many years I have been working on this project, I have accrued many debts of many kinds, intellectual, institutional, and personal. Among those who offered their help along the way, I am especially grateful to my colleague, co-teacher, and friend Jonathan Prude, who listened, talked, corrected, nudged, and teased this into a better book than it would otherwise have been. At various stages in the evolution of this work, Elizabeth Blackmar, Wai Chee Dimock, Ellen Gruber Garvey, Michael T. Gilmore, T. Walter Herbert, Myra Jehlen, Ruth Perry, Shirley Samuels, and Mark Selzer offered valuable advice and encouragement. For the friendship every writer needs, I can only thank Cynthia Enloe, Cristine Levenduski, Judith Rohrer, and Joni Seager.

My colleagues in the Graduate Institute of the Liberal Arts and the many graduate students with whom I have worked at Emory University have all left their marks on this project. I am particularly grateful for the interest, the insights, and the material assistance of Bryan Garman, Nancy Koppelman, Adrienne McLean, and Elizabeth West. Emory's University Research Council provided much-needed time for the writing of this book.

Emma and Daniel Lang contributed far more than they know to this book. Beyond time, patience, and cups of coffee, their conviction of the value of this project kept me at work, their commitment to social justice gave its subjects immediacy, and their belief that this project would end gave me hope. For sharing my home and my history during the writing of this book, I thank Julie Abraham.

The Syntax of Class

Introduction

CLASS, CLASSIFICATION, AND CONFLICT

I<small>N</small> 1851, the *North American Review* published a series of articles on political economy written by its editor, Francis Bowen, a man who would later assume the post of professor of natural religion, moral philosophy, and civic polity at Harvard. "There is a danger," Bowen wrote, "from which no civilized community is entirely free, lest the several classes of its society should nourish mutual jealousy and hatred, which may finally break out into open hostilities, under the mistaken opinion that their interests are opposite, and that one or more of them possess an undue advantage, which they are always ready to exercise by oppressing the others."[1] In Europe, as the revolutions of 1848 had amply demonstrated, the danger of rising class consciousness was a clear and present one. But not so, according to Bowen, in the United States, where the "mistaken opinion" that classes stood opposed to one another could only be held by those who failed to appreciate the "peculiar mobility" of American society, the continuous displacement of master by man which tended, in Bowen's view, to blur, if not altogether obliterate, the boundaries separating the interests of the "several classes" of society.

Properly considered—considered, that is, not in the light of Old World histories but of New World teleology—the existence of class divisions in America need not, Bowen insisted, signal antagonism, much less open hostility. In the absence of social distinctions sanctified by law or custom that "nothing short of a miracle" could change, the language of class was merely descriptive, identifying the broad social groupings natural to "civilized" communities. These groupings might be hierarchical in their arrangement, but in the American context they were entirely fluid in their composition. As Bowen used it, the language of class did not define a field of conflict where opposed interests would inevitably find expression in the political arena, or in the streets; on the contrary, he uneasily claimed, class provided neutral terms of official social description: it mapped the way stations along the route from pauperism to wealth open to each white, male American. Far from being irreconcilable, the interests of owner and laborer, master and man, like those of present and future, necessarily coincided as the latter lived in anticipation of the day when they would replenish the ranks of the former. The mobility of individual men would, in short, guarantee the harmony of interests of labor and capital and, by all rights, render the United States immune to the class warfare that wracked midcentury Europe.[2]

Bowen was neither the first nor, certainly, the last proponent of what has come to be known as the doctrine of the harmony of interests, nor was his the only effort to deny the political saliency of a language of class. In the context of an emerging taxonomy of class that newly acknowledged the existence in America of broadly homogeneous social categories, his appeal to individual mobility in the interest of excising the prospect of class conflict was, in fact, reiterated by influential elites throughout the nineteenth century. But the tenacity of Bowen's argument was matched by the tenacity of the fears it sought to allay, fears that were greatly exacerbated by what appeared to members of the newly consolidating middle class to be growing evidence of class antagonism. By the time of the 1849 Astor Place riot, the sarcasm of Francis Grund's 1839 *Aristocracy in America*—"Why sir, this is a republican country; we have no *public* distinction of classes"[3]—had already given way to portentousness. Reporting on the bloody confrontation between the "aristocracy" and the "people" outside New York's lavish opera house, the *Philadelphia Public Ledger* announced that "There is now in our country . . . what every good patriot has hitherto considered it his duty to deny—a high class and a low class." Interpreted in many quarters as a manifestation of the rising "hatred of wealth and privilege" provoked by the "unjust distribution of the avails of industry,"[4] the Astor Place riot made clear the civic danger that might attend a classed society. The language of class, as even Bowen's anxious insistence on harmony suggested, was no neutral taxonomic tool. To publicly admit the reality of class in America was to open the nation to the threat of class conflict.

That an unjust distribution of the "avails" of industry had, in fact, divided their world into a "high" and a "low" class could hardly have escaped the notice of urban Americans. The enormous concentration of wealth in the hands of a few—by some estimates, more than half of the nation's wealth was held by 5 percent of the population by 1860—and the concomitant impoverishment of the many was a conspicuous feature not only of the older urban centers of the Northeast but of the new cities that proliferated along the transportation routes opening the Midwest to a flood of immigrants and young native-born men seeking employment. By 1850, the journalist-flâneur George Foster, famous for his voyeuristic glimpses of New York "by gaslight," not only knew that the "wicked and wretched classes" existed but regarded it as the "duty of the present age" to "discover the real facts of [their] actual condition . . . so that Philanthropy and Justice may plant their blows aright."[5]

Whether or not they embraced the duty of their age, middle-class Americans were appalled at the circumstances of the poor and were frightened, too, by accounts of an urban underclass among whom, according to the American Bible Society, "crimes against society are plotted, and the most savage passions stimulated to action."[6] Prompted to ameliorative action, middle-class volunteers, many of them women, went into the slums to distribute tracts and Bibles, enroll children in Sunday schools, and minister to the destitute. Professionals and businessmen formed organizations to address the moral depravity and the looming social threat they ascribed to the poor. These organizations, like others of their kind, claimed that "A class more dangerous to the community . . . can hardly be imagined" than the "wretched" and "degraded" population of slum dwellers.[7] Even the sympathetic Charles Loring Brace, founder of the Children's Aid Society, was unambiguous about the danger that lay incipient in the urban poor, imagining the inevitable "herding together" of street boys whose eventual consciousness of their power would lead them to lay waste to the city.

In a social world routinely, if sensationally, represented as divided between "millions" and "mills," "fashion" and "famine," or, in Lydia Maria Child's words, "magnificence and mud, finery and filth, diamonds and dirt,"[8] the failure of traditional modes of social description to accommodate new social and economic relationships heightened public awareness of class differences. But so too did the ranging of those differences across terrain already marked out by ideologies of race, gender, and ethnicity greatly complicate the rendering of these new relationships. The language of poverty and wealth did not address the new self-consciousness that prompted chattel slaves to forecast their liberation by laying claim to the titles of "man" and "woman," or encouraged feminists to recast women as "citizens," or disposed angry white workers to describe themselves, however reluctantly, as "slaves." As the spread of a market economy and the shift to industrial modes of production proletarianized the trades, as the "slavery of wages" confounded categories of labor and race alike, as abolitionists and women's rights advocates claimed new social and political identities for slaves and women, as traditional customs of deference fell away, and as urban disorder of all sorts increased, middle-class fears of conflict called both the nature and the saliency of long-standing vocabularies of social difference into question.

The emphasis on social taxonomy in the treatises of political economists like Bowen, the strategic deployment of moral vocabularies in the reform tracts of Brace and his allies, and George Foster's effort to disaggregate the poor into the "wretched" and the "wicked" all reflect both the new awareness of class distinctions among Americans at midcentury and the increasingly problematic nature of social classification. In the quarter century following the revolutions of 1848, legislators, journalists, ministers, labor leaders, political radicals and fledgling political scientists, playwrights, and novelists would struggle to find a social vocabulary adequate to the task of naming, ordering, interpreting, and containing the effects of class difference in a period that saw not only the emergence of new social groupings and new kinds of people but one in which new class formations challenged the ideals of traditional republicanism and political democracy.

Not only Bowen's *North American Review* but other such influential journals as *Merchant's Magazine and Commercial Review* and *Southern Quarterly* devoted their pages to articles on "Abuses of Classification," "The True Theory of Labor and Capital," and "The Distribution of Wealth," while the *Democratic Review* printed titles like "Poverty and Misery, versus Reform and Progress." Elsewhere, in sketches like *Harper's* "The Factory Boy" or Fanny Fern's *New York Ledger* tale "Cash" and in illustrated papers featuring bootblacks, street toughs, Bowery b'hoys and their brazen g'hals, Broadway Brummels and black dandies, journalists and artists labored to delineate new social types. Reformers like Brace wrote tracts urging the employment or, in the case of girls, the domestication of the "dangerous classes," while sensationalists like P. H. Skinner detailed their violence in novels like *The Little Ragged Ten Thousand* (1853). In the increasingly class-segregated theater, "Mose," the volunteer fireman, brought working-class audiences to their feet, and pageants of city life like "The Seamstress of New York" (1851), "Katy, the Hot Corn Girl" (1854), and "The Rag-Picker of New York" (1858) joined the most famous and long-lived of the working-girl melodramas, Francis S. Smith's "Bertha, the Sewing Machine Girl, or Death at the Wheel" (1871). Minstrel shows, in the meantime, used blackface and transvestism to negotiate the complexities of class and ethnicity for the entertainment of white workingmen.

Likewise, from the faded aristocracy of the house of the seven gables to the orphan girls of domestic fiction, from the exploited factory operatives and domestic servants to the street "arabs" and the beleaguered free blacks who take center stage in midcentury novels, the fiction of this period recorded the deep unease that attended the naming of class in the United States. It is with these last that this book is concerned.

The Syntax of Class explores the literary expression of the crisis of classification that occupied public discourse in the mid–nineteenth century. It focuses on a group of novels written, like most novels, by middle-class city dwellers, in this case by American women and men living, almost without exception, in the urban Northeast. Their particularity lies in the fact that they tell stories of people who are not—or are not yet, or are never to be—themselves members of the middle class. Explicitly, as an element of the narrative itself, or implicitly, as a condition of their production—or both—these novels entail a definitive encounter between members of different classes.

The novels under consideration here are not offered as representative of the mass of fiction of this period, although in many respects they typify, as a group, the genres, narrative formulae, and social concerns that held the attention of the genteel reader. Reformist in their impulse and protorealist in their form, however, these novels are, for the most part, familiar ones, recently "recovered" from historical oblivion of one sort or another and much taught. Commonly understood to belong in one or another of the "alternative" canons structured along the axes of race or gender, they are read accordingly: the plight of the female artist, the problem of marriage, or the tragedy of the mulatto supplanting wage slavery, cross-class community, economic mobility, or "proletarianization" as the subjects of scholarly consideration. Class, that is, is rendered the largely invisible third term in critical discussions that claim race, class, and gender as their heuristic terms. The unevenness of these readings is no accident, nor does it represent a critical failure. On the contrary, as I hope to demonstrate, it mirrors the representational quandary confronted by midcentury writers of "social fiction."

The title of this study comes from Elizabeth Stuart Phelps's *The Silent Partner*, at the end of which the middle-class narrator observes a "syntax" in the "brown face and bent hands and poor dress and awkward motions"[9] of Sip, the mill girl. An orderly arrangement of terms indicating mutual relationship, a syntax is, on the one hand, contentless, and on the other, essential to the making of meaning. What follows is a series of experiments in reading, in parsing the syntax of class in midcentury fictions. These experiments are framed on one side by the uneasy attention of midcentury authors to class, and on the other by the equally uneasy elision of class from current critical discourse. My object is not to capture the full range of novelistic expression at midcentury, but rather to explore in close detail the formal negotiation of the complexities of class difference in particular novels written in a period in which the adequacy of social taxonomies and the implications of new class formations were sharply at issue. My aim, that is, is to think about how, precisely, distinctions of class are rendered in midcentury novels, and how, in turn, those renderings circulate in and through a larger cultural discourse about the dangers of class conflict.

I begin from the assumption that social taxonomies and novelistic representation are intimately connected and, moreover, that the instability of the former inflects the latter. Insofar as the conventional characters of a society inhabit its narratives and comprise a body of representations variously embraced, repudiated, debated, and deployed in the actual struggles of historical actors,[10] that body of representations has itself to

be made and has, moreover, to be made, if not out of, at least with reference to, the available discourses of social identity. This is, in one sense,
only to suggest the obvious constraints within which the novelist works—
even the eccentric must be recognizable as such. It is not, however, to
assume that writer and reader are in prior agreement about which of the
available social vocabularies is appropriate to the representation of social
difference, much less that reader and writer share a set of "common social
properties." Rather, like Gareth Stedman-Jones's political actors, writer
and reader are together engaged in constructing a representation both of
those shared social properties and of the social identities of others.[11]

To say, then, that *The Syntax of Class* concerns the negotiation of class
in a set of historically specific narratives that hinge on cross-class encounters is to say two quite different things. First, it is to assert that the contests
over the meaning of class I have sketched above—over both the anterior
social reality the language of class seeks to capture and the social prospect
to which it points—frame the novelistic representation of class difference.
But beyond this, it is to argue that the body of representations produced
in the novels under discussion here not only shape and are shaped by the
experience of class but actively participate in the process of articulating,
mediating, and displacing class difference and managing class conflict.

A number of difficulties attend a project of this kind. Perhaps the most
obvious one concerns the status of the language of class itself in the culture
of the United States. It has been argued that, however "real" the structure
of class in America, Americans have no "native discourse" of class in
which to render their experience of that structure. Lacking a vocabulary,
as it were, in which to express the experience of class—its complacencies
as well as its injuries and its struggles—and deeply committed, moreover,
to liberal individualism and the promise of open mobility, Americans displace the reality of class into discourses of race, gender, ethnicity, and
other similarly "locked-in" categories of individual identity. This displacement, in turn, distorts sexual and racial relationships by redistribut-
ing conflicts of class across these other domains.[12] Whether or not the
language of class is "native" to Americans—and certainly, elite theorists
like Francis Bowen expressed considerable anxiety about the appropriate-
ness of its use in reference to the republican United States, while other
midcentury Americans emphatically laid claim to class identities—such
patterns of displacement and their concomitant distortions are evident in
the construction of social identities and the representation of cross-class
engagement in the midcentury novels under discussion here.

It is by now more or less axiomatic in literary critical circles to assert
both the reciprocity and the incommensurability of the categories of social
identity that have proven most fruitful in literary studies and most salient

in the political arena. Class is understood neither to subsume nor to diminish the impact of race, gender, or ethnicity—in some arenas, it is arguably "defeated" by the material or subjective impact of these others[13]—nor are these others seen consistently to subsume class. Instead, imbued with the determinants of class, these categories of social difference are increasingly regarded as at once mutually constitutive and internally fractured. Class and its consciousness are, to paraphrase Cora Kaplan, more polymorphous and more perverse than we once imagined them, and the language of class less stable.[14]

But our willingness to see the displacement of class into the discourses of race and gender or, alternatively, to argue that class permeates representations of racial or gender difference has not led us to recognize the uneven use and the differential effects, the particular distortions and the social—as well as the literary—consequences, of those relocations of class. We acknowledge, for example, that the mutually defining character of the interlocked vocabularies of race, class, and gender is obscured in fiction as social identities come to appear self-evident. But we fail to recognize that, that being so, the production of social identities in novelistic (or political) discourse may nonetheless give precedence to one vocabulary of representation over another in the interest of achieving particular ideological ends—and likewise in literary critical discourse.[15] Writing in inequality, we write out power. Paradoxically, given the broad recognition within literary studies of the complex interconnection of ideologies of race, class, and gender, much literary scholarship elides class and its conflicts and ignores their displacement into other domains of social difference. To parse the syntax of class—to identify the ordering of language that makes apparent the mutual relationship of parts in which meaning inheres—is, then, I hope, to open a discussion of the impact of differentials of wealth, power, and prestige on the representations Americans make of and about themselves, a discussion endlessly deferred both in their literature and in the study of that literature.

The intricacy of that syntax is made evident in the effects apparently discrete vocabularies of social description have on one another. Thus it is that, set against the putatively neutral backdrop of the all-white social world of the domestic novel, the transformation of a barefoot "orphan" into a "girl" both sets the problem of the material inequities of class and sets it aside, producing, through the turn to gender, a woman who by meeting the gendered specifications of the middle class gains its material comforts as well. The whiteness of that penurious avatar of the middle class is hardly incidental to her fate—or that of others. Instead, it helps to accomplish the blackening of those thoroughly proletarianized figures whose gender cannot save them from the ravages of class—the factory operative or the mill girl. And the blackening of the working class, in turn, inflects the narratives of free blacks, where class position, however lofty, offers no defense against racism.

The uneven displacement of class across discourses of race and gender in the production of social identities in the novel has, then, multiple effects. But so too, in the historical moment with which I am concerned, does this pattern of displacement and the concomitant fracturing of class serve widely different ideological functions. In a novel like Maria Cummins's *The Lamplighter*, for example, the pain of poverty and the potential explosiveness of class difference alike are mediated through the figure of the impoverished orphan whose carefully cultivated "womanliness," by apparently springing her loose of class, simultaneously confirms her rightful position in the middle class and locates the promise of social harmony in her well-ordered home. By contrast, the blackening of the wage "slave" in industrial fiction, by underlining the worker's lack of mobility, intensifies the prospect of class conflict—and constrains it too. Insofar as he—or she—is represented as shackled by class and morally disfigured by it as well, the wage slave is, like the chattel slave, at once safely immobilized and deeply threatening. The injuries of class that are naturalized in the "brown" face of the white weaver and the female "sobriquet" of the male millworker are rendered irremediable and their consequences, both social and individual, incalculable. Yet in a novel like Frank Webb's *The Garies and Their Friends*, the blackening of the proletariat and the proletarianization of blackness reiterates the effects of racism, heightening, on the one hand, the import of class status in interracial interactions and erasing, on the other, the antagonisms of class within what W.E.B. DuBois called the "community of blood and color prejudice." Framed by the exclusion of African Americans from the social and political, if not always the economic, benefits of class mobility and written against the cultural backdrop of widespread and multiform racist caricature, nineteenth-century narratives of free blacks offer systematic and self-conscious accounts of the production of social difference across the intersecting grids of class and race. My point, perhaps by now obvious, is that the syntax of class structures the kaleidescopic displacement of terms of social difference and generates the figures—the orphan girl, the free black, the millworker—through whom the experience of class and its antagonisms are managed in American novels.

If the status of the language of class in the United States and the syntactical complexities of fictional representation constitute the first difficulty of a project of this kind, a second difficulty that besets such a project is how to think about the nineteenth-century middle class and, by extension, class itself. Like most novels, those under discussion here must, with perhaps the single exception of Harriet Wilson's *Our Nig*, be characterized as speaking both from and to the middle class. In one sense, that is only to say that the view they offer across the lines of class is mediated, shaped, and constrained by the material conditions of authorship and literacy in the nineteenth-century United States. But as the continuing debate over the ideological work of the novel in constituting, expressing, debating, subverting, or policing middle-class hegemony and the more recent recognition of the internal fracturing of class along the lines of race, gender, and ethnicity alike suggest,[16] to describe the novel as embedded in the middle class is neither to fix the relationship *between* the novel and the middle class nor, for that matter, to locate in any very precise way what we mean by the middle class. In fact, in literary discussions of the ideological work of the novel, the term "middle class" is most often used as a kind of shorthand to point to the privatistic and entrepreneurial values of a historically—and often geographically—unsituated bourgeoisie, or, in the American case, to a broad national culture of liberalism. Despite the varying stances of novelist or narrative, the competing social views expressed in fiction, and its sometimes subtle subversions of the claims of liberal individualism, the novel is generally taken to be the definitive literary genre of the "middle class" by virtue of its focus on individual self-making in the fluid social universe generated by a market economy, even in those American narratives where that enterprise is thwarted by the impact of racial and gender inequality. This assumption of the intimate, if politically unpredictable, relationship between the novel and the middle class in American literary scholarship has, for the most part, arisen independent of and without reference to the ongoing historiographic debate over the existence of the middle class in the United States as a distinct social formation.

Most closely resembling the view propounded by the "consensus school" of American historians typified by the work of Louis Hartz, the understanding of the middle class that predominates in scholarship on American literature posits a middle class so "triumphant" that it not only "[takes] itself for granted" but frames and articulates a possessive individualism so widely embraced as to be the common property of Americans regardless of their place in the scheme of production or, indeed, of consumption.[17] But if the liberalism of the "consensus" historian's middle class so thoroughly infiltrates American culture as to be indistinguishable from it, the incoherence of a class bearing no stable or definable relationship to the means of production has rendered the middle class at best transitional and at worst artificial from the vantage point of the classical Marxist. To those historians focused on the persistent framing of conflict—especially political conflict—along the deep divides of race, ethnicity, and religion, the force of class divisions in the United States has appeared sufficiently diminished as to be of little explanatory value. Nonetheless, recent historical scholarship on working-class and patrician culture in the United States as well as the work of those like Burton J. Bledstein, Mary P. Ryan, and Stuart M. Blumin on the emergence of the middle class have made it increasingly evident that the deep economic inequalities of the mid–nineteenth century produced not only widely divergent life circumstances but a middle class whose beliefs, aspirations, and ways of living and working were definitive, a bounded middle class aware of itself as distinct from both the rich and the poor in its interests, its values, and its styles of life. In this scholarship, the "middle class" identifies neither the horizon of American culture—the commonly held and widely diffused system of conduct and belief that delimits a national community—nor a grouping so economically incoherent or politically incidental as to obviate the possibility of its coming to consciousness. Rather, it points to a social formation whose coherence lies not in the consistency of its productive relations but in a complex of economic circumstances and cultural convictions delimited enough to produce among its members a self-awareness sufficient to reinforce class boundaries, not erase them.[18]

A class paradoxically bound together by its "common embrace of an ideology of social atomism" and prone to "express its awareness of its common attitudes and beliefs as a denial of the significance of class,"[19] the nineteenth-century middle class that emerges from the work of Blumin and others neither insists on its identity as a class nor does it, for the most part, function politically—and antagonistically—as an interest group. In the absence of the usual evidence of class consciousness and of the significance of class affiliation in political conflict, historians have turned to demonstrable changes in the character and experience of work, in family strategies and organization, in customs of deference and styles of self-presentation, in residential patterns, and in patterns of consumption at midcentury to argue for middle-class formation. The characteristic, even definitive, denial of class by the nineteenth-century middle class and its concomitant unwillingness to admit the existence of the values, interests, beliefs, and ways of living embraced by those of other classes, much less to credit these, might be seen, not surprisingly, to inform the work of those like Francis Bowen who invoked the language of class only to deny its force as well as those who repudiated it. Certainly it informs the fiction of this period. And as the range of novels to which literary critics devote their attention has expanded to include not only the narratives of promising young men but those of women, workers, and nonwhites, the effects of middle-class denial of the impact, if not the existence, of class has become peculiarly problematic for the literary scholar.

Despite the loosing of the narrative of middle-class formation from the exclusive realm of productive relations by Blumin and others, the historians' account of the emergence of the middle class shares the masculinist tendencies characteristic of historical (and sociological) discussions of class and, it must be said, of most genre-based discussions of the novel and the middle class. Just as, until quite recently, the study of "race" meant the study of African Americans and the study of "gender" meant the study of white women, so in the study of class the "real" subject has been, almost without exception, white working-class men. The shift of focus to the middle class has not significantly altered that gender bias, and neither, interestingly, has E. P. Thompson's crucial insight into the "making" of class in historical relationships that exceed the workplace in their form and their expression.[20] The exclusion of the mental and productive lives of working women has, Carolyn Kay Steedman forcefully argues, distorted the "monolithic story of wage-labor and capital";[21] likewise, for all their apparent centrality to the story of middle-class formation in the United States, the experiences and the subjectivities of middle-class women have been generalized into relative insignificance in the historical account of class—or split off into a history framed around the imperatives of gender.[22] Engaged as women are in "making" gender, their participation in the "making" of class is regarded, it seems, as incidental. Thus despite Blumin's acknowledgment that the formation of the middle class and the concomitant production of new social identities entailed not only the realignment of work and workplace relations but "events. . . in the 'separate sphere' of domestic womanhood," and even that "to this extent, middle-class formation was women's work,"[23] the activities and experiences of men remain at the center of his analysis of the urban middle class in the nineteenth century.

Yet it would seem, in no small measure, that if the distinctively middle-class embrace of liberal individualism is best captured through an examination of the public lives of men, so the equally characteristic denial of the saliency of class is tightly bound to a cultural preference on the part of the emerging middle class for the rendering of class distinctions through the cultural vocabulary of gender difference. I do not, of course, mean to suggest that these two aspects of middle-class formation belong exclusively to one sex or the other. Rather, I want to suggest that the elision of class in the literary critical discussion of American fiction is not unrelated to the skewing of the historical account of the rise of the middle class toward a masculine public sphere.

Though largely excluded from the historical narrative of middle-class formation, women—particularly white, middle-class women—figure prominently, by contrast, in the current narrative of American literary history. Yet the female authors, readers, narrators, and characters of mid-nineteenth-century American novels whose positions on the grids of race and gender are so carefully charted by literary scholars appear in the narratives those scholars produce to be free of class, to be transcendent figures whose middle-classness is a consequence of—or at least inseparable from—their womanliness and their whiteness. Class, that is, collapses into gender and race in the literary discussion of these novels, and, more important for my purposes, the middle class appears there not as a specific or bounded class formation but as a blur of spiritual or religious ideals, domestic virtues, and standards of comportment more readily ascribable and more regularly attributed to gender ideology than to class position. By setting aside a historical narrative of middle-class formation in which women figure only incidentally, late-twentieth-century literary critics succumb to the sleight of hand of mid-nineteenth-century novelists, reproducing in their analyses the cultural logic of the novels themselves.

That "home" has emerged as a central term in the discussion that follows is a trace effect of the central role of the middle-class woman in the negotiation of class and the mediation of class conflict in midcentury novels. But precisely insofar as middle-class homes—"homes, in the better sense"—figure as the loci of social harmony, the meaning of home reaches far beyond the domestic setting to capture what is lacking and what is to be desired, what has been lost and what is to be gained in the navigation of class. In the public discourse of midcentury America, as now, home signifies refuge from the exigencies of the market-world. It stands as the antidote to history, a utopian site in which "changes never come," in which the deeply conservative values—the "family values"—ascribed to women rightfully hold sway, in which heterosexual union figures a larger social harmony. In this sense it stands, too, as a figure for a racially homogeneous and putatively classless national community from which African Americans are excluded and in which the interests of women need not be represented, so clearly are they "daguerreotyped" on the hearts of men.
But in the heterogeneous discourse of fiction, these senses of home are joined to others that extend, reframe, literalize, metaphorize, and challenge them. The claims of African Americans to a "home" in America, like their representation of the racial community as home, stand in defiance of a nation that would leave them orphaned and homeless. The "orphaning" of the child of the street is made evident by the disorder of the tenement in which she lives, even as her whiteness and her femininity secure her inheritance of a home of the very best kind and a respectable genealogy as well. The anti-homes of the proletariat, the dank cellars and dirty hovels into which factory operatives and millworkers retreat at night, like the lineage houses of the would-be aristocracy in which the value of real estate is absolute and domestic art has no scope, portend their doom. In the circle of "friends" separately established by men and women, the antagonisms of class that inflect heterosexuality are resolved through the creation of homes founded on the harmonious ground of gender solidarity.

Figured, then, through the home, within the home, between homes, in the absence of homes, and in the creation of new homes, engagement across the boundaries of class in the novels under discussion here is as thoroughly domesticated as it is conflicted.

By looking at the novelistic rendering of cross-class encounters in a historical period characterized by the emergence of a public discourse of class and the simultaneous consolidation of a middle class inclined to deny the efficacy of class itself—and likewise its threat to social harmony—I intend to bring the specificity of middle-class formation to bear on the formal consideration of mid-nineteenth-century American novels. My object is to argue for the value of a nuanced and historically informed use of class as a category of analysis in literary studies. But it is also, and more importantly, to propose that the same structure of displacement and deferral that organizes—and problematizes—the literary representation of class supports an ongoing political culture in which the all but universal claim to membership in the middle class is exploited by those in power to void the necessity of addressing the appalling extremes of wealth and poverty that characterize twenty-first-century America.

Chapter I

HOME, IN THE BETTER SENSE

The Model Woman, the Middle Class, and
the Harmony of Interests

I~N~ 1850, New York's first chief of police, George Matsell, announced that he had uncovered a "deplorable and growing evil." The "constantly increasing" army of "idle and vicious children of both sexes, who infest our public thoroughfares," he announced in his semiannual report, was not merely the symptom but the veritable source of crime, disease, and disorder in the city.[1] By the time of Matsell's report, the offspring of the newly named "tenement classes," long the objects of charitable attention, had already been recast in the imagination of the middle class as evidence of a growing and uncontrollable underclass. Even as intervention of a variety of kinds was urged, the danger with which these children were invested was drawn with unusual candor by reformers like Charles Loring Brace, founder of the Children's Aid Society. Banding together in the city streets, boys "form an unconscious society," he argued, on the basis of which, as men, they will "come to know their power and *use it*!" More explicitly than most, Brace acknowledged that the danger that lay incipient in the street urchin was that of class consciousness. "If the opportunity offered," Brace predicted, "we should see an explosion from this class which might leave this city in ashes and flood."[2] "Cunning and adroit," these "half-naked, dirty . . . leering children," driven from the tenements by want and overcrowding, were reputedly confirmed in vice: they begged, stole,[3] and fought; they drank, gambled, and prostituted themselves; they spread depravity and disease. Barely recognizable as "part and portion of the human family,"[4] they were scarcely children at all.

The omnipresence of these ragged urchins on the streets highlighted their ambiguous humanity. For if street urchins barely belonged to the "human family," they seemed, more immediately, to belong to no family at all. They were, in the insistent phrase of the Children's Aid Society, "orphans," "friendless and homeless." According to Christine Stansell, such children were rarely orphans in fact, and even when they were, they were generally neither "friendless" nor homeless. Yet one suspects that the insistence on their orphanhood by police, politicians, and reformers

alike reflects neither ignorance nor bias but, on the contrary, the commitment of these middle-class observers of tenement life to a particular understanding of what constitutes a home, an understanding framed by the
rapidly consolidating culture of domesticity. In their view, the "dark,
filthy hovels" of the poor made a mockery of the word itself: as one such
observer pronounced, "Homes—in the better sense—they never know."[5]

Of course, the question of what constitutes a home "in the better sense"
was not only of interest to male reformers and politicians. It was equally
of concern to the women, most of them white and middle class, who
wrote and read the scores of domestic novels published at midcentury. To
both, one thing was clear: "home" was the antithesis of the overcrowded,
disorderly, inharmonious tenement inhabited by the unruly poor. If the
tenement was, in a striking displacement of the language of domesticity,
"the parent of constant disorders, and the nursery of increasing vices,"[6]
the "home," overseen by an ideally nurturing mother and supported by
a just and industrious father, was, as novel after novel insisted, a veritable
nursery of virtue, producing the modest daughters and the promising sons
of the emerging middle class. Like the vast, undifferentiated expanse of
empire that, among other things, allowed for the transportation of street
"orphans" to the rural West to find their fortunes, the narrow and highly
ordered literary space marked out as home "in the better sense" was designed to contain the danger of class antagonism. The scope of the first
was understood to ensure social harmony by its broad promise of "opportunity" for mobile young men; the containment, even constriction, of the
latter offered domestic novelists an image of social harmony organized
around ideas, not of mobility, but of constancy, in which the conflicting
interests of history could be resolved in the harmonious relationships of
the conjugal family. The teleology of progress was, in both cases, made
immanent in a particular projection of space. In domestic novels like
Maria Cummins's *The Lamplighter* and Nathaniel Hawthorne's *The
House of the Seven Gables*—the works under discussion here—the well-
regulated home served not merely as a refuge from the fluctuations of
men and markets but as a bulwark against social strife.

Early in Susan Warner's best-selling *The Wide, Wide World*, one of the
urtexts for critical discussions of domestic fiction, young Ellen Montgomery's mother articulates the domestic ideal toward the achievement of
which these novels were directed. Home, in the best sense, as Mrs. Montgomery explains on the eve of her separation from her daughter, is a place
"where changes never come."[7] Her husband's fortune at risk, Mrs. Montgomery is about to depart for Europe, where she will die, and the "home"
to which she alludes is heaven, where partings like that between herself
and her daughter "cannot be."[8] In the ever-narrowing scheme of the
novel, however, the constancy of that heavenly home is reiterated, first,

in the image of an ideal domestic setting, a perfectly ordered home in which love is abundant, money sufficient, and residence permanent, and then, in the woman of the house, whose piety, patience, affection, and unending generosity remain constant when all else fails. When the inconstancy of men or market disrupts the outward order of the home, that woman turns to a self the perfect mastery of which figures an ideal order. Thus the young Ellen's prolonged and painful education in the appropriate expression of emotion, submission to legitimate authority, and Christian piety, in the proper preparation of tea and a mindful consumerism—an education essential both to the harmony of the home she will someday oversee and likewise to her spiritual reunion with her mother in heaven.[9]

Warner's configuration of nineteenth-century domestic ideology as an aspect of the female self—what Richard Brodhead describes in more limited terms as the introjection of the mother[10]—suggests not only what historians and literary critics have long noticed, that is, the conflation of the feminine and the domestic in the antebellum period, but, more particularly, the ideological affiliation of women and order in a period of disconcerting social "changes." As I hope to demonstrate, in works as superficially different as *The Lamplighter* and *The House of the Seven Gables*, the self-possession that marks the middle-class woman holds change, history, and, with history, class conflict at bay.

Homes in all their variety offered reformers and politicians an easy ground for social differentiation: children too much on the streets were "orphans"; the tenements of the poor were a mockery of home not only because of their putative lack of moral and physical order but because their communalism and their open doors compromised their status as "private" space; the laboring mother or child violated what Stansell has called "the moral geography of family life" as this was understood by the middle class: "men at work, women at home, children inside."[11] If in the official discourse of what we might call public disciplinary culture—the culture represented by men like George Matsell and Charles Loring Brace—that mockery of home, the tenement, stood as a crucial sign of the lower classes, so for the middle-class culture of domesticity, home "in the better sense" was the emblem.

Karen Halttunen has persuasively argued that mid-nineteenth-century sentimental culture, of which domestic fiction is a central articulation, served as "an unconscious strategy for middle-class Americans to distinguish themselves as a class while still denying the class structure of their society," "to define themselves against the lower classes even as they insisted they were merely distinguishing themselves from vulgar hypocrisy."[12] To press Halttunen's point, the middle class was "aware," as Anthony Giddens would have it, but not "conscious" of itself as a class.

Unlike class consciousness, the awareness of class does not entail either the "admission" that to hold class-specific attitudes and beliefs is to "signify a particular class *affiliation*" or, for that matter, the "admission" that other classes, characterized by other attitudes and beliefs, exist. On the contrary, as Giddens argues, class awareness may "take the form of *a denial of the existence or reality of classes.*"[13] The emphatic commitment to individualism of the American middle class as it figures in midcentury domestic narratives suggests just such a denial of the reality of classes if by that we mean that class position is not credited as definitive or that the beliefs and the lives of those above and below are regarded as untenable, inadequate, or morally flawed. But these narratives, with their attention to urban poverty, rural self-sufficiency, and fashionable hypocrisy, deny the efficacy of class in a particular way. Embracing an alternative system of classification centered in the home, domestic narratives use gender difference, rhetorically and ideologically, to order the disorderly engagements of class, to obviate the necessity of class consciousness.[14] And insofar as domestic narratives employ the protocols of gender to harmonize differences of class in the creation of a normative middle class, they participate fully in what has been called "*the* sentimental fiction." They rely, that is, upon the myth that the sentimental domestic project is undertaken in the interest of individual self-control not the control of others, and certainly not those classed and racialized others who provide what Laura Wexler has dubbed the "human scenery" against which the perfect self-possession of the middle-class woman is made visible.[15]

At midcentury the middle class was, as it were, in rehearsal. Even as powerful advocates of the doctrine of the harmony of interests of labor and capital insisted on the illusory nature of class conflict in the forward march of American industrial capitalism and urban observers pointed to a single great divide between the profligate (or philanthropic) rich and the vice-ridden (or worthy) poor, the middle-class home gained a special status. Disguised by "the scrim of ideology that venerated gender difference,"[16] it was understood to be a place outside class, crucially, a private place, in which the task of inculcating the ideals of female self-control and male self-creation essential to membership in the emerging middle class would proceed under the close supervision of the mother, insulated from the disorderly world outside.[17] This privacy, increasingly insisted upon in antebellum formulations of the "separate spheres" of men and women, all but defines the sense in which the middle-class home was understood to elude class. The integrity of the middle-class home, in other words, may have lain in the fact that it was dominated not by relations of class but by those of gender, but the gender norms so carefully instilled in that home were nevertheless thoroughly conditioned and inflected by class. In this sense, domestic fiction is, of course, all about class.

My point, however, is a different one: namely, that the ideological un-
derpinnings of home "in the better sense" in gender not only reflect class
affiliation but enable the *negotiation* of class relations and distinctions.
Set between the mansions of the fashionable rich and the hovels of the
miserable poor, the middle-class home is offered in domestic fiction not
as a location *in* class—requiring as that does a relative understanding of
class as a bounded formation—but as a place in which the effects of class
are so thoroughly mediated by an alternative paradigm of gender, the
object of which is to produce a condition of classlessness, as to disappear
from view.

The sign of successful membership in the middle class in domestic novels lies squarely in the capacity of the female protagonist to elude classification, to take possession of an ideal self putatively outside class—and
therefore outside history—and thus able freely to negotiate the divergent
social universes of the rich and the poor. By this I mean both able to move
physically through the various quarters of the city without harm and able
to negotiate the emotional effects of the wealth and squalor to be found
there.[18] The socializing strategies of the middle class, so minutely illustrated in domestic novels, are offered, then, not only as evidence of middle-class superiority or coherence but also as an answer to the problem
of class itself. Ostensibly freed from the burden of class—by virtue of
her transcendent spiritual commitment, or her "disinterestedness," or her
innocence of history—the ideal woman at the center of the domestic novel
simultaneously figures the possibility of classlessness and exposes the reality of class difference. Propagating what has been described as "a large-
scale depersonalization of those outside its complex specifications" while
magnifying and flattering "those who can accommodate to its image of
an interior,"[19] she offers in every way an "interior" of the better sort.

The story domestic novels tell is, then, the story not of moving up but of
moving out of class, the story, that is, of the production of the woman
whose radical self-possession places her outside history, outside the play
of interests—economic, social, and political—that render the world unstable. The problem of producing such a woman is set with remarkable clarity in the opening chapters of Maria Cummins's 1854 best-seller, *The
Lamplighter*. The novel opens outside an "unwholesome-looking" tenement boardinghouse on a "close street" in one of "those neighborhoods
where the poor are crowded together."[20] The evening is "chilly," snow is
falling, and eight-year-old Gerty, an "orphan" of mysterious parentage,
is sitting, barefoot, on the stoop. Left by the death of her mother in the
charge of her hardworking but vicious landlady, Gerty is barely fed and
often beaten. Having neither employment nor schooling, she spends her
days on the streets and at the docks, alternately railing and weeping at

ply and answer one another; to think about the kitten is to remem-
shoes, but it is also to find a solution in kittens to the problem of
t.

urns out, of course, gender is not entirely what it seems but rather
alternative account of class. No native daughter of the tenements,
instead, as we later learn, the child of eminently respectable par-
gnorant and undisciplined as she is, Gerty has a genetic proclivity
genteel, intimated early in the novel by "a something" in her "na-
at keeps her aloof from the "rude herd" of street urchins (216)
the "sanctum" she creates for herself in the local woodlot, a
of sorts in which she weeps as mightily as any Ellen Montgomery,
fferent reasons. In light of the eventual revelation of her origins,
e could regard the maternal feelings elicited in Gerty by the help-
en—but, significantly, absent in her landlady—as a sign of the
nd social gulf that separates the vicious lower classes from their
But these are not the terms on which the narrative proceeds. In-
y cannot be, insofar as the story Cummins is offering is about the
on of the problem of class conflict through the production of an
domestic woman—insofar, that is, as Cummins recruits gender
service of harmonizing the class differences implicit in the opening
ory. Gerty's besetting problem, then, is the getting (and keeping)
s—the getting, that is, of physical comfort, maternal affection,
c order. For to have shoes is, in *The Lamplighter*, to have a
and to have a home one must, if a girl, love kittens.

's progress, in other words, depends on a strategy of displacement
h the vocabulary of class yields to that of gender, in which the
ns of poverty are answered by the apparent naturalness of the
." The problem of poverty is not repressed but rather translated
cabulary that makes its redress possible, if not inevitable. In the
at have come to be conventional in discussions of domestic fic-
rty's story is that of a worthy but impoverished orphan girl's rise
ctability through her own strenuous effort and the combined good
f the generous poor and the charitable rich. But set in motion by
in the terms of Gerty's identity from poor to female, from the
of not having shoes to the problem of having a kitten, the narra-
cts our attention to the relationship between these categories. Its
ifts seamlessly from an incipient concern with social justice to the
tly more urgent need for the reform of individual character, the
nt of which will, in turn, yield a more perfect justice.

's affection for the kitten both establishes her right to a proper
d provides her with the means to get one. Joining the ranks of
hy poor to which Trueman Flint belongs, Christy immediately
er schooling in liberal Christianity, self-control, and the domestic

the injustice of her lot and suffering the ta
who, in an encounter prior to the opening
shoes into the harbor.

The shoeless Gerty is pathetic, but she i
bad. She is, in fact, the very image of the un
belligerent, profoundly ignorant, unwashe
rags, she is "the worst-looking child in th
haved" (213) as well, prone not only to the
tic of the girl protagonists of domestic nove
acts of violence. Yet before the first chapte
befriended by the sympathetic local lamp
whose name matches his matchless charact
suffers at the hands of Nan Grant, Flint tal
ises to "bring her something" when he retu
evening. Needing everything, Gerty spect
thing" might be: "Would it be something
shoes! But he wouldn't think of *that*" (21

And indeed, he doesn't. The "something
a kitten, a gift that leaves Gerty in a quand
lives, the narrator mildly observes, "there
though Gerty finds the kitten appealing, sh
were most grudgingly accorded to herself
tended to her pets" (218). Nonetheless, th
is clear. The kitten elicits a maternal and
tenderness notably absent in her working-c
wise belligerent Gerty. It indicates, that i
fitness to move out of her deprived and de
doxically, prompts her worst behavior. G
the kitten quickly provoke a violent confro
unfeeling landlady, in the course of whic
entire lack of maternal feeling, drowns t
Gerty, giving vent to her rage, hurls "a sti
her strength" (221), drawing blood. Cast
now homeless and still shoeless Gerty is t

In this brief opening episode, class is
visible by gender. In lieu of the continger
or collective, Cummins invokes the essenti
of true womanhood. No abstract or litera
The Lamplighter is, rather, a problem of m
the problem of who does and who does n
is immediately tied to the matter of gender
as the lens through which substantial ine
the other, obscures its origin in class. Th

both in
ber the
bare fe

As it
itself a
Gerty i
ents.[21]
for the
ture" t
and by
"closet
if for d
then, o
less kit
moral
betters.
deed th
resolut
ideally
into the
of her s
of shoe
domest
home—

Gerty
in whic
distorti
"woma
into a v
terms t
tion, G
to respe
offices
the shi
probler
tive dir
focus s
appare
fulfillm

Gerty
home a
the wo
begins

arts. She is removed from the "blows, threats, and profane and brutal language" (214) of Nan Grant into the circle of "disciplinary intimacy"[22] composed of True and his female confederates, where she will grow not merely into a woman but into "a model to her sex" (501). In anticipation of that transformation, Gerty's first act, on rising from the sickbed to which her shoeless sojourn in the snow has remanded her, is to create a parlor. Provided immediately with shoes, not to mention a "dark, calico frock," she institutes a regime of domestic order unknown in the chaos of Flint's bachelorhood with the tactful assistance of Trueman Flint's "quaker-like" neighbor, Mrs. Sullivan. Sweeping, scrubbing, tidying, and, most crucially, moving the beds out of sight, Gerty creates within Flint's single room the intermediate space between the public street and the private quarters of the family that, in sentimental culture, signals the presence and influence of women.

If the tenement in which Gerty begins is a mockery of home in the better sense, Flint's newly organized room is an adumbration of that home, indicating the developmental trajectory of Gerty's story. Unfitted as yet by age and education to ascend the "cultural podium" of the "real" middle-class parlor,[23] the child Gerty signals her future role as moral and social arbiter by creating what might be seen as an infantile or primitive version of that parlor. But Gerty's interior decorating is only as important as her interior experience of it. Physical comfort and social aspiration of a modest sort dictate the reorganization of Flint's room, but the pleasure attendant on that reorganization is the pleasure of pure altruism: the creation of the parlor, like her care of the kitten, brings Gerty a "happiness— perhaps the highest earth affords—of feeling that she had been instrumental in giving joy to another" (234). Even as Gerty burns the toast and breaks the teacups, her domestic diligence and her affection for Flint come together to initiate a disciplinary regimen that will ultimately yield a perfect alignment of inner and outer selves.

Without the altogether disinterested pleasure it brings her, Gerty's capacity to create a pleasing domestic order would be of little consequence. For the point here is not simply to produce in Gerty a proper respect for the outward forms of the middle class but to produce subjectivity of a particular sort. Her initiation into genteel styles of living elicits and ratifies structures of feeling that will free her of the constraints of class altogether. The object of female education in *The Lamplighter* is not only to move Gerty out of the slums but to get the slums out of Gerty. Insofar as this entails emotional reeducation, Gerty's case is not altogether different from that of Ellen Montgomery, whose genteel and loving mother has, from the outset, ensured her mastery of the rituals of afternoon tea,[24] the pleasing arrangement of furniture, and the tasteful choice of clothing. But unlike Ellen, Gerty must learn to check a set of impulses and behaviors not merely unfeminine or unchristian but explicitly antisocial, impulses and behaviors understood by everyone around her to have been inculcated by tenement life and to represent the danger of "orphans" like her: a thirst for revenge that leads her to hurl bricks through Nan Grant's windows, a readiness to defend Trueman Flint's dignity from the jeers of her schoolmates with her fists. Self-consciousness, in other words, is to occupy the psychic space that might otherwise have been occupied by class consciousness. The end point of the scheme of female education in domestic fictions is to learn to take delight in serving others and to cultivate a self-control so perfect that it allows the protagonist to "bear even injustice" (292) with patience and good temper.

What is figured in the urchin Gerty is the prospect of a masculinized rebelliousness founded in material deprivation, a class consciousness that frames the problem of bare feet precisely as one of social injustice. Although she is no "confirmed pugilist," Gerty nonetheless acts like a boy, and not insignificantly, for the danger of the street urchin—overwhelmingly a male figure despite the ungendered term—lay in his propensity to violence. Without access to an economic arena in which to fulfill the promise reformers like Brace saw in them, boys of the street were imagined to be active agents of social disruption and potential agents of class warfare. Variously pathetic or dissolute, girls, on the contrary, were believed to be more manageable; if only they could be made to feel and act like girls, they could save the class-divided city from doom. In fact, through the domestication of such girls, appropriate gender norms might be established for both sexes and the social geography of the city reformed.

There is, then, in Gerty's case a covert displacement of terms as well as an overt one: to go from poor to female, from shoes to kittens, is also to go from male to female, insofar as the bad behavior of the poor is almost invariably represented as masculine behavior. In order to get the shoes she so desperately needs, Gerty must submit, albeit willingly, to a thoroughgoing resocialization; in order to merit those shoes, she must learn to be governed by feminine love, not masculine rage. But to repudiate the self formed in rage at her shoelessness is not only to repudiate her particular class history and her boy-self but, as it turns out, to move outside of history altogether, to inhabit a world of kittens.

Like her guardian angel, Emily Graham, who is "shut out from the world" by her blindness and therefore "safe from worldly contagion" (531), Gerty is, in a different sense, shut out from the world, having no rightful place in it. Together they cultivate not Fashion but "feeling," not Society but "composure." Blind Emily, spiritually enlightened by her literal plunge into darkness, is insulated by her father's wealth from the necessity of acting in the world. Living in near seclusion, she is an innocent, simultaneously a "child of nature" (531) and a perfect Christian.

With her spotless white dresses, her unearthly calm, and her complete submission to the will of God, Emily embodies the feminine ideal toward which Gerty learns to aspire. But Gerty, who must keep herself in shoes, can only approximate this ideal by other means. The frail and wealthy Emily, with the composure of a saint, has risen above the world altogether—she is, in her fragility, poised perpetually on the threshold of heaven—but the impoverished Gerty's "composure" is a necessary adaptation to her social dislocation, though it renders her likewise invulnerable to the vagaries of fashion, the vices of poverty, and the fluctuations of fortune that characterize the social universe of the novel. Dependent on the Grahams for both shoes and kittens, subsistence and affection, but an orphan nonetheless, Gerty must achieve both spiritual and economic independence—an independence that turns out not to be a mere self-sufficiency but an entire freedom from the impositions of class.[25]

The angelic Emily represents an ideal womanhood, but she is not the only point of comparison Cummins offers in tracing Gerty's growth into womanhood. At one extreme of the developmental continuum—and the class structure—of the novel stands the working-class shrew, Nan Grant, the antithesis of all that Gerty is taught to admire. Brutish, foul-mouthed, so ill-tempered a wife that she has driven her husband to a life of seafaring and so lax a mother that her son has taken early to crime, Nan Grant is the product of want and ignorance. Her only virtue is her capacity for a drudgery that yields neither the inward pleasure of altruism nor the outward semblance of domestic comfort. As is conventional in domestic fiction, at the opposite extreme stands the stock figure of "Fashion," whose recurrent presence in domestic novels marks the unacceptable upper limit of social aspiration for the protagonist. In *The Lamplighter*, this function is served by the selfish, petulant Belle Clinton, whose self-importance is matched only by her material extravagance. Class does not invariably make the woman, as the figures of the wealthy but angelic Emily Graham and the poor but self-sacrificing Mrs. Sullivan demonstrate, but the model woman in *The Lamplighter* is nonetheless neither working-class nor fashionable. In fact, the "woman" is the antithesis of these not merely by virtue of her conduct but because the position she occupies is divested of social saliency. Unlike the drudge or the belle, whose places in the scheme of social classification are clear, the point of the "woman" is that she has no particular class location; despite her perfect conformity to the gender prescriptions of the middle class, her attributes are presented as unclassed, ahistorical.

The vocabulary of gender is structurally able to displace that of class because the attributes—racial, sexual, spiritual, occupational, temperamental—that define class position are rendered either so intrinsic or so transcendent that they pass either below or above history. The street orphan thus rewritten into true womanhood becomes then the figure of a world without "changes," without history, and without conflict. For if the potential for social conflict emerges as the contingency of social status is acknowledged, that potential disappears as the space between the attributes that are taken to constitute class—and in which an explanation of their conjunction might be undertaken—vanishes. The doctrine of the harmony of interests, of which this is the literary analogue, subsumes difference into one harmonious whole by means of a kaleidescopic substitution of terms.

In order successfully to negotiate—and elude—the class-bound universe of the novel, Gerty must thread her way through a complex web of possible identities—not only angel, drudge, and belle but, as we learn in a climactic moment in Gerty's life with the Grahams, slave and lady. Faced with conflicting obligations, Gerty defies her generous but despotic benefactor, Mr. Graham, in order to fulfill what she deems a higher duty, founded in love and secured by her promise to Willie Sullivan, her "brother" and future husband, to care for his ailing mother and aged grandfather. Furious at Gerty's decision to leave his household and take a job teaching school, Mr. Graham re-orphans Gerty, as it were. Expelling her from his home before she can leave of her own accord, he expostulates to his daughter: "She prefers to make a slave of herself in Mr. W's school, and a still greater slave in Mrs. Sullivan's family, instead of staying with us, where she has always been treated like a lady" (326). Of course, Mr. Graham is wrong, for as the reader knows, Gerty chooses to "enslave" herself, and that choice, arising out of love, transforms slavery into a form of freedom. Fully in possession of herself, she cannot be bought or sold; she can only, as it were, give herself away. In Mr. Graham's lexicon, however, the laboring woman, whether a paid teacher or a volunteer nurse, is a "slave" and not a "lady," although even he realizes that Gerty is not, in fact, a "lady" but merely "treated like" one, not a "daughter" but an orphan. Emily, by contrast, understands that to sacrifice the self out of love, without regard for the "world," is not subordination but the highest form of independence: it is, precisely, to be neither a "slave," subject to the will of others, nor a "lady," oblivious to the needs of others, but rather a "woman," a free agent whose moral determinations (and thus behavior) are unencumbered by her economic status, just as the terms of her identity are sprung free from the system of social classification that names ladies and slaves.

Of course, Gerty's move to the city also demonstrates her economic independence, the ability to earn a living at which her education, as Emily points out to her father, was aimed. "Enslaving" herself to Mr. W's school and to the needy Mrs. Sullivan, Gerty is liberated, briefly, from her status as a dependent—a "slave" who is "treated like a lady"—in Mr. Graham's household. Indeed, intermixed with her righteous sense of an emotional obligation fulfilled and a promise kept is Gerty's satisfaction at her ability "to earn a maintenance" (331) for herself. Lest we confuse economic independence with spiritual independence, however, Gerty readily forfeits both her pride and her newfound self-sufficiency—her salary and the "beautiful" rented room into which she moves after Mrs. Sullivan's death—to her "sense of the right" when the tyrannical Mr. Graham, promising to restore her to "the place and appearance of a lady" (360), summons her to the failing Emily's side. This sacrifice, undertaken out of love rather than social ambition, nonetheless restores to Gerty the protection of a "father" and the comforts of his well-appointed home.

It is hardly surprising that the language of slavery, the irreducible social difference against which all others are measured in this period, finds its way into *The Lamplighter*. Nor, given the racializing of class in midcentury novels, is it surprising that color figures in the orphan's transformation, however incidentally. Gerty—whose complexion, we are told, is "dark" but "clear" (317)—suffers from a "dark infirmity," a sinful because violent rage at injustice that is simultaneously the emotional sequela of tenement life and the trace effect of a masculinizing poverty. A register of her identification with those who suffer "ill-usage and neglect," the "dark infirmity" of her class history must be cured if Gerty is to become "a model to her sex." As the example of blind Emily suggests, the promise of Christianity is the promise that darkness will be supplanted by light, sin by salvation, rage by love. But just as Gerty's "dark infirmity" is tied to her slum origins, the light of Christianity, in what is perhaps, in 1854, an inevitable slide into racialized language, is figured first in the white plaster figure of a praying child-Samuel, a perplexing "white image" given her by Trueman Flint and cherished by Gerty even before its meaning is expounded by Willie Sullivan. The cultivation of the orphan Gerty's "natural"—that is, feminine—capacity to act out of love rather than a masculinized class anger, then, establishes her position not only in gender but in race as well. By paying her "debt to society" in the coin of "universal love" (362), the ambiguously sexed urchin Gerty, who hates "old, dark, black places" (250), becomes the woman Gertrude and is "whitened" as well.[26]

With no claim by birth or fortune to a place in the world of the Grahams and nothing in common with the "rude herd," able to "earn a maintenance" (331) for herself but retaining a perfect spiritual autonomy even when economically dependent, the adult Gertrude is apparently formed outside the social world altogether, out of the "natural" materials of gender and race. Unmarked by class and in this way perfectly middle class, she occupies a position of social intermediacy that allows her to travel freely between class locations, which are, in turn, spacial renderings of her developmental trajectory. From the tenement to Trueman Flint's modest single room at the back of the building to the Graham's elegant but tasteful townhouse to rented quarters in the city and, finally, to a home of her own with Willie Sullivan at the close of the novel—each domestic relocation signals her ever-greater "composure," her more "complete self-control," her "independence" of the class-bound world. That perfect command of the self leaves her equally at ease entertaining guests in the parlor of the Graham's bucolic summer house and ironing Emily's dresses in its kitchen, in Mrs. Sullivan's modest dwelling, in fashionable Saratoga among the representatives of "the best society" (444), or in the crowded tenement flat where she ultimately discovers the dying Nan Grant. Claimed as a "daughter" by the bachelor Flint, the penurious Mrs. Sullivan, and the affluent Mr. Graham alike, Gerty acts the part to all of them but belongs to none. With her modest manners, her "neat" and "simple" dress, and her complete self-control, she moves between city and country, parlor and tenement, not untouched—for remembering her own suffering, her sympathies are readily engaged by that of others—but impervious to the slights both of those who think her too lowborn to merit their regard and those who disdain her as an "upstart." Just as the kitten replaces (and provides) the shoes in the first episode of *The Lamplighter*, Gertrude's womanliness, summoned by the kitten and cultivated throughout the novel, substitutes for the social position we understand her to lack, a position that is, however, magically secured in the end when we discover that Gerty is no orphan after all but the daughter of the prosperous and eminently respectable Philip Amory, the long-lost fiancé of her spiritual mother, Emily Graham.

The reconstitution of the family through the marriage of Gerty's "true" mother and actual father in the final chapters of *The Lamplighter* gives Gerty a hereditary right to home, but it also complicates Cummins's narrative. The affection for kittens that brings Gerty shoes, while bound rhetorically to her gender, is, as it turns out, predicted by if not predicated on her class of origin, the effects of which are, in turn, represented as being as "natural" as a love for kittens. Only the synergy of gender and class, it would seem, can produce the model woman whose good taste and capacity for affection are, equally, "inborn" and whose "dark infirmity" is an accidental effect of her accidentally impoverished childhood. But having the right to a home and having a home marks the difference between promise and fulfillment, between children and adults. In order to gain a home of her own, Gertrude must not merely recover her family of origin but also marry and found a family of her own.

The new family thus established is, however, likewise revealed to be a reconstituted one when Gerty marries Willie Sullivan, the son of the woman who calls her "daughter." Represented first as Gerty's "brother" when, as children, they live side by side at the back of the "decent two-storied house" (223) to which Trueman Flint brings the urchin Gerty, Willie is an exemplar of the "promising" male self on whom the narrative of economic progress depends—a commodified self, continually buying shares in his own future, whose improvement reflects both "innate privilege" and "moral obligation."[27] Thus possessed of himself, he is, of course, the rightful partner in marriage of the orphan girl who, being a girl, need not purchase her future but only own it. The son of the admirable Mrs. Sullivan and her husband, an "intelligent country clergyman" (241) whose early death has plunged his family into poverty, he combines the privilege conferred by parents whose respectability is secure, however reduced their circumstances, and a moral conviction that he must not merely "support and comfort" his mother and grandfather but fulfill the great hopes they have of him. Willie's largely invisible rise from poverty to prosperity depends on a utopian marketplace in which the cycle of production and consumption is completed within the compass of the individual who "buys" the idea of his own future and sells it as well. Entailing the perpetual motion of the futures market, the promising Willie's ascent from shop boy to clerk to small capitalist, while it both parallels and complements Gerty's ascent to model womanhood, is apparently accomplished in radically different terms. Yet Willie's reclamation of his hereditary status suggests that the advancement enabled by the utopian marketplace is, like Gerty's advancement by adoption, ensured by birth. Like the girl's, the boy's story too carries him out of history by undercutting the narrative of striving with one of inheritance.

Nonetheless, "promising" is precisely what a girl—particularly a girl from the slums—must not be, implying as it does her sexual availability. There is no utopian marketplace for the model woman; for her, commodification signifies moral compromise, and consumption excess appetite. Yet in a different sense, the orphan Gerty is, of course, the most promising self of all. On the one hand, she is a girl who loves kittens, and her progress to womanhood is natural and inevitable, given a home; on the other hand, she is free from the impositions of class insofar as these are taken to originate in the family she lacks—or, alternatively, entirely shaped by her "real" but invisible class origins. Her rhetorical "orphaning" makes her available for adoption into a home "in the better sense" that is in any case her birthright. Saved by her womanliness from the streets, where lack of self-control might render her a sexual commodity—a "promising" girl—and by her economic dependence from the world of fashion, in which selfish extravagance reflects a similar failure of self-regulation, Gertrude "has no money in her pocket, but her soul is the pure gold" (501). The introjection of the market essential to the success of the promising Willie—that model of possessive individualism—is precisely what must be resisted by Gertrude, for whom, as commodity or consumer, engagement with the marketplace invariably represents not upward mobility but moral decline. Yet it is in the joining of these two—the "pure gold" of the womanly Gertrude's soul with the actual gold in the promising Willie's pocket—that home in the best of all senses originates.

In one way, then, Willie and Gerty's parallel development is essential to the outcome of Cummins's novel. In another way, however, the narrative of Gerty's growth into spiritual self-possession on which the energies of the novel are expended might be seen as supplanting—and suppressing—the more problematic story of the impoverished Willie's economic rise. The social threat represented by a Gerty is readily dispersed by the rhetorical move from orphan to girl; no such neat rhetorical solution is available to contain the threat of the poor boy. If that threat is to be obviated by his "promise," the rhetorical sign of the marketable conviction of his future success, the world must offer him scope in which to rise. Yet as I have already suggested, the narratives of Willie and Gerty alike turn out to be narratives not of advancement but of recovery, not of mobility but of inheritance: both claim their future by birthright. In keeping with that perfect harmony in which "changes never come," all the "changes" that set the plot in motion—Gerty's "orphaning," Willy's poverty, Philip and Emily's separation—are reversed as all individual histories recapitulate one another. Even the "changes" in social status we believe to have been accomplished through the strenuous effort of the meritorious are revealed as simply the recovery of what has fallen out of their grasp. In the symbolic economy of *The Lamplighter*, nothing actually changes. No loss is permanent, everything can be recuperated: parents and children, "brothers" and "sisters"—not only Willie and Gerty but also Philip and Emily, likewise raised as siblings—are reunited; the financial losses of the previous generation—most notably, those suffered by Philip Amory's father and Willy's mother—are reversed; lovers are rejoined and, by marrying, reconstitute families disrupted by death and misfortune. Not mobility, then, but stability, the reconstitution of a lost gentility, is the end point of the narrative of domestic progress, the boy's rise and the girl's constancy.

And just as the acquisition of home brings Gerty's history to an end, so too home arrests history more broadly by fulfilling its promise, by providing, in the fullness of time, the harmonious domestic space in which love reigns and all interests are one. For the motive and the object of the economic ambitions of the novel's promising young man—like that of his older benefactors, the "self-made" Misters Clinton and Graham—is not, it turns out, ceaseless advancement but rather respite from striving, figured in a home where changes do not come. With all the empires of the world from India to "Arabia" in which to make his fortune, the successful Willie yearns not for "doubtful honors" or "precarious wealth" but for "rest," "a peaceful, happy home, blessed by a presiding spirit so formed for confidence, love, and a communion that time can never dissolve, and eternity will but render more secure and unbroken" (502).

The only view we are offered of the interior of the home Willie and Gerty establish at the end of *The Lamplighter* is that of its parlor, "well-lit, warm, and pleasantly furnished" (550). The location of that home, however, receives considerably more attention, for it is apparently on the very street where they first met in poverty. Their window, a front window now, looks out on "an old brown building—the same corner building which had been visible from the door-step where Willie and Gerty were wont to sit in their childhood" (550).[28] From this comfortable but modest urban dwelling, they can, quite literally, observe the distance they have traveled. This recuperation of childhood is consonant with the larger recuperation of family that characterizes the ending of the novel. But it is also problematic, suggesting as it does that nothing, not even the revelation of their heredity, can get Gerty and Willie out of the old neighborhood. Although Philip Amory removes with his bride to a "mansion-house . . . the property of [his] paternal grand-parents," using his "ample means" to "judiciously modernize" the "venerable homestead" (551), his daughter Gerty seems to have a claim on neither means nor mansion. And indeed she can have none, not only because the reinstatement of patrilineal privilege would undermine the meritocratic structure of the novel, but also because Gerty's most important inheritance is matrilineal, albeit metaphorically so: the inheritance of a proper femininity. Her status as orphan or daughter need not be addressed, because her claim to the title "woman" is secure. In fact, the revelation of Gerty's genteel parentage is entirely anticlimactic, telling us only what we already know from a far more reliable source, her spiritual history. The revelation of her class of origin is only the proof of her classlessness, the reprise of the past only proves the justice of the present, and a knowledge of history only confirms the righteousness of outcomes.

·   ·   ·

The investment of a novel like *The Lamplighter* in detailing the production of the model woman lies in the capacity of that woman to provide a counterweight to the highly unstable antebellum social world. "Home" there is something like a projection in space of the woman whose introjection of the virtues associated with the rising middle class—female self-control, domestic privatism, benevolent maternalism, Christian forbearance—is so complete that she is "at home" wherever she goes. Providing both the motive and the reward for the labors of her promising young man, as we have customarily understood it, the model woman—the embodiment of perfect constancy—and the interior she creates offset the fluctuations of the market world in which he strives for advancement even as they actively lend themselves to his success.

All this being so, I want nonetheless to propose that the overwhelming emphasis in domestic novels on the synonymous values of self-control, self-possession, "composure," "independence," and "poise" has a far broader import than this, that in fact, self-control and social control are conflated in the figure of the model middle-class woman in this fiction. A perfect command of the self is, of course, essential to framing "a home where changes never come," but it also grants the model woman immunity from history. The standard against which she is measured, and measures herself, is the "pure gold" of womanliness and not the unstable currency of the social universe. She is, that is to say, invulnerable to that historical world in which others are constrained by fashion or famine. And just as she is released from the strictures of class, so the home she creates in her image designates a social space as perfectly stable as her own identity and equally unmarked by invidious distinctions of class. Figuring the utopian possibility of the transcendence of class itself, she figures as well a social order without conflict—as conflict-free as she herself learns to become. Disallowing by its very structure the possibility of class conflict, the vocabulary of gender enables the social fantasy of an unbounded and uncontested mobility essential to the creation of a normative and generalizable middle class.

In light of this ideological function, the wholesale appropriation of the figure of the model woman in *The House of the Seven Gables*, Hawthorne's gothic tale of the last days of a doomed aristocracy, makes a different kind of sense. Patrilineal inheritance and venerable old mansions stand at the center of *The House of Seven Gables* and are, as a rule, understood to translate the domestic novelist's sentimental absorption in the question of home into the severely masculine one of real estate. I want here to carry my reading of the domestic novel against the ground of class formation to what is nonetheless the most "domestic" of Hawthorne's romances. I want, that is, to examine the way an attentiveness to class plays out in a novel where masculine understandings of home as lineage and as property dominate and where interactions between men are essential.

The problem of *The House of the Seven Gables* is how to make a "home" in the ruins of the House of Pyncheon—how, that is, to release the present from the haunting crimes of class that have entangled Pyncheons and Maules since that "by-gone" age when the aristocratic Colonel Pyncheon, through a combination of "personal influence," "iron will," and legal manipulation, stole the land of the obscure artisan Mat-

thew Maule and called down upon his lineage the curse of choking to
death on their own "blood," on their dynastic pretensions. The confusion
that leads Clifford Pyncheon to conflate "roof and hearth-stone," terms
held to "embody something sacred," and "real estate . . . the broad foundation on which nearly all of the guilt of this world rests"[29] is arguably
the confusion the novel aims to resolve. Setting the "private and domestic
view" of women against a masculine public one, the truth of "pencil
sketches that pass from hand to hand" against the false appearances of
"portraits intended for engraving," The House of the Seven Gables, like
The Lamplighter, proposes that the answer to class conflict lies in the
purified relations of gender.

That, in any case, is the implication of the novel's notoriously unsatis-
factory ending. The marriage of Hawthorne's model woman and her
promising young man unwrites the dark history of the Pyncheons and the
Maules: the hereditary curse is broken, the crimes of class are tran-
scended, and the energy of a new democratic age is celebrated in the marriage of the versatile and idealistic Holgrave to the competent Phoebe.
The fall of the House of Pyncheon is complete, down to the spontaneous
destruction of the portrait of its progenitor, and in its place rises a vision
of "home." Just as the virtues of domesticity replace the value of property
and as conjugal love supplants patrilineage, so the newly constituted Pyn-
cheon-Maule family, harmonizing all interests by its interclass character,
will, we are led to believe, sweep away the last vestiges of "ancient prejudice." Lest we doubt this outcome, the newly harmonious relationship of
the classes is echoed in the "strain of music" provided by the spirit of
"sweet Alice Pyncheon." As the music swells, the new lovers and their
antiquated cousins depart the death-ridden mansion to take up residence,
"for the present," in the "elegant country-seat" they have conveniently
inherited from Jaffrey Pyncheon, the avatar of the family's evil genius.

Other signs, however, are less auspicious: the Pyncheon elm whispers
"unintelligible prophecies," and Maule's Well throws up "kaleidoscopic
pictures" of the future that only a "gifted eye" can see. The fate of the
conjugal family is, as T. Walter Herbert has convincingly shown, ambiguous at best.[30] And so too is the capacity of the unnamed middle class it
exemplifies to unwrite the history of class. The trouble with the ending
of The House of the Seven Gables is voiced by one of those rough "laboring men" whose function throughout is to comment on the Pyncheons'
activities: "Well, Dixey . . . what do you think of this? My wife kept a
cent-shop . . . and lost five dollars on her outlay. Old Maid Pyncheon has
been in trade just about as long and rides off in her carriage with a couple
of hundred thousand—reckoning her share, and Clifford's and Phoebe's—and some say twice as much! If you choose to call it luck, it is all
very well; but if we are to take it as the will of Providence, why, I can't

exactly fathom it!" (318). Of course, "Old Maid Pyncheon" is not "in trade," nor is her newly acquired wealth the product of her labor. Nevertheless, Dixie's friend has a point: the "lower classes," as Hepzibah styles them, seem always to lose on their investments, while the aristocracy, whose demise the novel ostensibly recounts, are fortuitously saved from poverty, not by the "will of Providence" but by patrilineal inheritance. Spoken with bemusement but without "hostility"—that "only real abasement of the poor"—the laborer's aside marks the limits of the social transformation that separates the present from that "by-gone" time when the "aristocracy could venture to be proud, and the low were content to be abased" or at least "kept their resentments within their own breasts" (25).

In the new age of physical and economic mobility, of endlessly fluctuating fortune, rank has lost its saliency. As Holgrave explains to Hepzibah, while urging, with "half-hidden sarcasm," the merits of abandoning the "circle of gentility" and joining instead in "the united struggle of mankind" (45) with "necessity" (44), "these names of gentleman and lady" belong to "the past history of the world" (45). In the present, there are only men and women. The plodding tradesman and the "laborer in his leather jerkin" (12) are no longer remanded to the kitchen. Instead, they, along with the "hard, vulgar, keen, busy, hackneyed New England" women (48) who are their wives, their "urchin" children, the occasional Italian organ-grinder, and the sage but penurious Uncle Venner, rub shoulders with the gentry in the streets and feel free to comment on the affairs of their social betters.

But the new heterogeneity of the once "fashionable quarter" of Pyncheon Street does not mean that distinctions of wealth and power have fallen away. In the democratic present of the novel, "amid the fluctuating waves" that characterize social and economic life, the cunning performance of a false equality by the rich has replaced aristocratic arrogance. The "free and hearty manner" of a Jaffrey Pyncheon toward those more "humble" than himself bespeaks "a haughty consciousness of his advantages, as irrefragably as if he had marched forth, preceded by a troop of lackeys to clear the way" (130). Nevertheless, there is a difference between the old and the new: "hereditary" nobility is gone; "rank," now merely "the grosser substance of wealth and a splendid establishment," has "no spiritual existence after the death of these" (38). But the conventional distinction between the persistence of rank and the transitory character of class contributes in no small way to the laboring man's perplexity. The "public honors" and the political influence wielded by a Jaffrey Pyncheon cannot be bequeathed to his heirs; the "spiritual" substance of his status dies with him. But the actual wealth out of which it grows and to which it contributes, passed on to the next generation, both reifies the divide between rich and poor and ensures its continuance. The perfor-

mance of social equality that characterizes the new democratic age constitutes a change in form but not substance; it allows the laboring man freely
to voice his puzzlement, but it in no way alters the material relationship
between himself and the Pyncheons. His family is still out five dollars
while theirs inherits a hundred thousand.

Considered from the vantage point of the laboring man, the new social
order differs from the old largely by virtue of its greater mystification.
Whereas aristocratic privilege and the concomitant language of rank once
provided a plausible account of social and economic difference, the persistence of sharp divisions of poverty and wealth into the new democratic
age is, as the laboring man makes clear, unfathomable—and, the narrator
hints, more dangerous in direct proportion to its inexplicableness. The
contemptuous familiarity with which the "lower class" patrons of Hepzibah's cent shop address the impoverished gentlewoman and the hostility
it elicits in her—toward them and, paradoxically, toward the idle rich
among whom she can no longer count herself—stand as evidence of her
absurdly outdated aristocratic pretensions. But, like Holgrave's "half-hidden sarcasm" and Judge Pyncheon's patronizing smile, they also suggest
that neither the arrogance of the rich nor the rage of the poor can be
safely relegated to the past.

In fact, the staging and restaging of the "crimes" of the Pyncheons and
the Maules has the effect of bringing those crimes into the present of the
novel, of reminding us not only of the extension of their consequences into
the present but of the present potential for their repetition. That is to say,
it is not merely guilt that persists into the present but also inequality, and
insofar as this is the case, neither the depredations of the rich nor the
hostility of the poor can be wholly contained in the past. The Pyncheon
"family-mansion," built on the very "spot first covered by the log-built
hut of Matthew Maule" (9), in which nearly all the action of the novel,
such as it is, takes place, instantiates class conflict both because it gives
material form to the expropriation of the land—the "home"—of the
Maules and because its siting affords the "ghost" of the dead wizard "a
kind of privilege to haunt its . . . apartments" (9). The house of the seven
gables is, then, the locus of a conflict between wealth and poverty, promi-
nence and obscurity, that, unresolved and apparently unresolvable,[31] binds
generation after generation of Pyncheons and Maules to one another.

Generation after generation of male Pyncheons and Maules, that is:
Colonel Pyncheon, who "[wore] out three wives" (123), and the "wizard"
Matthew Maule, whose wife is nowhere to be seen; the effete and apparently widowed Gervayse Pyncheon and the virile bachelor carpenter Matthew Maule; Jaffrey Pyncheon, whose wife "got her death-blow in the
honey-moon" (123), and the unmarried Holgrave. Like Dimmesdale and
Chillingworth in *The Scarlet Letter*, who are united by a hatred that is

indistinguishable from love in its "intimacy and heart-knowledge," in its "passionate" need for its object,[32] these men are irrevocably bound together in an endless reenactment and recital of the crimes of their forebears. Each of them both possessed and possessor, they are obsessively involved with one another. Colonel Pyncheon not only occupies the homesite of Matthew Maule, as Maule's ghost occupies his, but engages Maule's son as its "architect"; Gervayse and the carpenter Maule conspire together, however uneasily, in the sacrifice of Alice Pyncheon; Holgrave, haunting the House of Pyncheon, presents himself to Phoebe by offering a daguerreotype of Jaffrey Pyncheon and declares his love for her only when Jaffrey is safely dead. I do not mean to imply a homoerotic connection here but rather to propose that male homosociality defines class conflict, that class conflict is offered as an intense form of relationship between men.

Neither the intensity of male entanglement nor the absence of women, as Eve Kosofsky Sedgwick suggests in the course of her exploration of the male-male-female erotic triangle, however, renders women inconsequential to this structure. On the contrary, as Sedgwick has argued, "the status of women, and the whole question of arrangements between genders, is deeply and inescapably inscribed in the structure even of relationships that seem to exclude women—even in male homosocial/homosexual relationships." The "inherent and potentially active structural congruence" between male homosociality and "the structures for maintaining and transmitting patriarchal power,"[33] to which she alludes, demands women for its expression. Illuminating as is Sedgwick's paradigm of a sexual rivalry in which men use a woman as the "conduit" for their keen interest in one another, I want to extend its terms in a direction intimated but not explored by Sedgwick. For the ambiguous status of the woman, as property and as sexual object, suggests her availability as the conduit for a class rivalry that, like sexual competition, binds men to one another. It is not only that the proper circulation of women in lawful alliance, like the "healthy circulation of property," must be accomplished in *The House of the Seven Gables*, as Teresa Goddu has rightly suggested.[34] The relations of inequality between men must be mediated by way of those alliances. Triangulated through the figure of the model woman, the apparently antithetical interests of men of different conditions can be harmonized—but only insofar as that woman's mediatory function vis-à-vis men and the mediatory function of the middle class she serves vis-à-vis extremes of wealth and poverty are collapsed into one.

Logically, then, "Alice Pyncheon," Holgrave's fiction of the laboring man's revenge, occupies a central position in *The House of the Seven Gables*. A powerful cautionary tale, it plays out the unsuccessful negotiation of class interests through a woman whose failure, as woman and therefore as medium, ensures tragedy. It provides, moreover, both an intermediate and an alternative account of the conflict between Pyncheons and Maules. Unlike the "legendary" account of the original conflict offered by the narrator in the prefatory first chapter, the interpolated story of Alice Pyncheon, ironically intended for "Graham or Godey"—women's magazines "programmatically dedicated to advancing the middle class and its values"[35]—is set in the eighteenth century and written by the last descendant of the Maules. Complicating the seventeenth-century story of land theft and wizardry—material and supernatural possession—by introducing sexual possession as the metaphor for these, "Alice Pyncheon" anticipates the importance of Phoebe, its protagonist's nineteenth-century descendant, as the figure of social harmony. In fact, it is precisely in the systematic *correction* of Alice's story that Phoebe's function becomes most clear.

One critical account of this correction proposes that the cross-class sexual attraction between plebeian Matthew Maule and aristocratic Alice Pyncheon, unacceptable in a pre-Revolutionary context, is redeemed in democratic times by the marriage of Holgrave and Phoebe. But Holgrave's fantasy of the revenge of the lower classes is far more complicated than this account suggests. The "bitterness" at "hereditary wrong" that metaphorically turns Matthew Maule's face as "black" as that of Scipio, the "black servant" who delivers Gervayse's summons, is matched by the hauteur with which the "foreign bred" Gervayse, a man of "artificial refinement," receives the "low carpenter-man" from whom he hopes to purchase the secret of the lost deed to Waldo County that he believes will ensure his fortune. As Holgrave tells it, every detail of the story—from the expensive "English sea-coal" Gervayse burns in his fireplace to his lace ruffles and embroidered vest, his French coffee, his Venetian antiques, and the Claude landscape that adorns his wall—exploits the difference between the Old World and the New to heighten the contrast between the social circumstances of Maule and Pyncheon. The encounter between the carpenter and the would-be "Earl of Waldo"—and Holgrave's fictional account of it—is fraught with class hostility, rendered in the conventional terms of the eighteenth century: bitterly identifying himself as the "grandson of the rightful proprietor of the soil" (194), the "brazen" Matthew Maule refuses to enter the house through the servant's door or to await Gervayse's convenience. Pyncheon, in turn, explains to him, with "haughty composure," that "A gentleman, before seeking intercourse with a person of your station and habits, will first consider whether the urgency of the end may compensate for the disagreeableness of the means" (197).

Despite Maule's "stiff" pride and Pyncheon's nonchalant arrogance, despite the hypermasculinity of the one and the effeminacy of the other, the two men strike a bargain: restitution of Maule's land in exchange for information leading to the recovery of the missing deed. Only, however, by means of an alternative exchange of property, through the "clear, crystal medium" of the virginal Alice Pyncheon, can this transaction be consummated. Unlike Phoebe, however, Alice is no model woman, although the "tender capabilities" of her sex are latent in her. She is, on the contrary, a "lady born . . . set apart from the world's vulgar mass by a certain gentle and cold stateliness" (201). Her cool appraisal of the comely Matthew Maule—the "witchcraft" of whose eyes, we are told, has not hitherto escaped the notice of "the petticoated ones" (189)—fuels his hostility and provokes what can only, given its highly sexualized language, be understood as a rape. His "evil potency" breaching the "sphere" of her womanhood, the "barriers" she believes unassailable, Maule, "standing erect" with his carpenter's rule "protrud[ing]" from his pocket, takes "possession" of Alice while her father averts his eyes.

Given the implicit sexual violence of this account, it is not surprising that Alice fails as a medium: her "pure and virgin intelligence" violated, she can provide no clue to the whereabouts of the missing deed. More important, however, the account of Alice's "possession" by Maule, suggesting as it does her unconscious complicity in her own violation, points to her failure as a woman. The "preservative force of womanhood" that should render her "impenetrable" is "betrayed by a treachery within" (203), by the "artistic admiration" (201), at once disdainful and desirous, that provokes Maule to vengeance. That betrayal of self, in turn, manifests itself in precisely the terms familiar from domestic fiction. Alice suffers from a complete loss of "self-control"; "possessed" by Maule, she is lost to herself. To lose "self-control," as novels like *The Lamplighter* make clear, is to lose the quality that most essentially characterizes the true woman and the one that crucially enables her mediatory role.

Alice is in equal parts the victim of the men who exploit her to negotiate an accommodation of their interests—a martyr to her father's desire to measure his land "by miles, instead of acres" (208) and the carpenter's "hereditary resentments" (195)—and of her own fatal willingness to pit "woman's might" against man's. Betrayed by her father and Maule and compromised by her ambiguous interest in the carpenter, she is doomed to live out her days in "humiliating" spiritual bondage and sexual thrall to Matthew Maule, who claims absolute possession of her—"she is fairly mine" (208)—though he leaves her in the "keeping" of her father. The effect of this possession, of her violation, is to exclude her from the office of woman; "So lost from self-control" is she that she deems it "a sin to marry" (209). But the lack of self-control that renders marriage a "sin" in her eyes is not the only or perhaps even the greatest obstacle to a lawful union: already "possessed" by a man, she is by definition unmarriageable. It makes sense, then, that Alice can be awakened from "her enchanted sleep" (209) only when Maule himself marries and takes legal possession of another woman, thus completing Alice's humiliation. Seduced and abandoned, Alice is released from bondage not to marry but—in the tradition of the eighteenth-century seduction tales it echoes—to die, "penitent of her one earthly sin, and proud no more!" (210). In Holgrave's rendering of her, Alice is, Clarissa-like, the appropriate heroine of her time as likewise is her descendant Phoebe.

In losing the self-control requisite to marriage, what Alice loses is the capacity to make a "home," the capacity most emphatically present in her descendant Phoebe, whose first act on the morning after her fortuitous arrival at the house of the seven gables is to "reclaim" the "waste, cheerless, and dusky chamber" (72) in which she has spent the night. Already possessed of the domestic skill Gerty must acquire just as she already epitomizes middle-class virtue, Phoebe, with "a touch here, and another there" (72), a vase of white roses and a judicious rearrangement of curtains and furniture, transforms the gloomy room into a "kindly and hospitable" one, and what is more, purifies it "of all former evil and sorrow by her sweet breath and happy thoughts" (72). The "process" of Phoebe's domestic art, the narrator tells us, is "impossible" to describe (72), but its effect is to make "a home about her" (141) wherever she goes.

And this is lucky since Phoebe needs a home, although she is no orphan. Displaced by her widowed mother's remarriage, she is nonetheless emphatically her mother's daughter, her "knack" for the domestic, like her skill at gardening and shopkeeping, transmitted entirely through her "mother's blood" (78). No foreign-born exotic but a native daughter of New England, Phoebe is everything Alice is not. Rather than a "born lady," she is the product of an interclass marriage between one of the Pyncheon cousins and a "young woman of no family or property" (24), from whom she "takes everything" (79). Indeed, in the estimation of her cousin Hepzibah, Phoebe is "no Pyncheon," despite her name, precisely as and because she is no "lady" (79). She is, instead, a "woman" and an "angel," "the example of feminine grace and availability combined, in a state of society, if there were any such, where ladies did not exist" (80). As one contemporary British reviewer astutely observed, Phoebe "must stand for the Middle Classes of Society, to whom has been committed by Providence the mission of social reconciliation which, once completed, the disunited are joined."[36]

Exhibiting all the virtues of middle-class femininity, Phoebe is imported directly from the domestic universe of works like *The Lamplighter* into the gothic world of the house of the seven gables just in time to avert the crisis of social classification prompted by her cousin Hepzibah's impoverishment. Phoebe's strategic arrival plays out in narrative form her larger ideological function. Reduced by necessity to engaging in trade, the tragicomic Hepzibah is the type of the "immemorial lady" (38) who feeds on "aristocratic reminiscences" (37) and believes that "a lady's hand soils itself irremediably by doing aught for bread" (37). Driven from her "strict seclusion" (31) into the "world's astonished gaze" (40) as the keeper of a cent shop, Hepzibah is both shamed and baffled to discover that not only the substance but the very terms of her identity have lost their meaning in the new social order. In the "republican country" in which she hopes to eke out a living, the "names of gentleman and lady," as Holgrave informs her, imply not "privilege, but restriction," but labor, he insists, will transform her from a "lady" into what is better, a "true woman" (45). And indeed the first copper coin she puts in the till has a galvanic effect, seeming to demolish in an instant "the structure of ancient aristocracy" (51). But the naturalized language of gender that replaces the ancient distinctions of rank in the new democratic age holds no promise for the antiquated Hepzibah, whose nearsightedness renders the present barely visible. Instead, Phoebe, arriving at the very moment of Hepzibah's putative transformation from "patrician lady" to "plebeian woman," relieves her cousin of the necessity of giving up her aristocratic delusions by taking over the housekeeping and the cent shop and by providing an alternative to both patrician and plebeian.

A Pyncheon without the aristocratic airs of her relatives, a New England housekeeper devoid of vulgarity, Phoebe in her perfect womanhood perfectly mediates between lower and upper classes. And she does so not only symbolically but literally insofar as she moves effortlessly[37] and unselfconsciously between the cent shop, the garden, the street, and the Pyncheon mansion, retaining her own identity intact. "Admirably in keeping with herself, and never jarr[ing] against surrounding circumstances" (80), Phoebe accomplishes what domestic fiction teaches us only the model woman can: she creates about her "that very sphere which the outcast, the prisoner, the potentate, the wretch beneath mankind, the wretch aside from it, or the wretch above it, instinctively pines after—a home!" (141). Her sympathetic presence harmonizes all differences, assuring everyone from outcast to social pariah to potentate that his "place was good in the whole sympathetic chain of human nature" (141).

In contrast to Alice's aloofness, Phoebe's "poise" reflects a perfect command of the self and protects her from the sexual and spiritual incursions to which Alice falls prey. Recoiling in modesty from Jaffrey Pyncheon's kiss, in which "the man, the sex . . . was entirely too prominent" (118), and unconsciously deflecting Clifford's sexual interest by her innocence,

Phoebe is betrayed by no "treachery within." Even when she is mesmerized by Holgrave's tale of Alice Pyncheon—when with "one wave of his hand and a corresponding effort of his will, he could complete his mastery over Phoebe's yet free and virgin spirit" (212)—her "individuality" and the reverence it elicits prevent Holgrave from exercising his power. Phoebe's "individuality" and, as we learn, Holgrave's "integrity" are alike evidence of the unified self that averts disaster. If Phoebe, unlike Alice, suffers no internal division, so too does Holgrave, unlike Matthew Maule, resist the temptation to "acquire empire" over a Pyncheon. Since they are driven neither by arrogance nor by rage, their responses, at this moment, originate neither in history nor in class but in "nature," that is, in gender. Just as Phoebe is utterly at home wherever she is, so Holgrave, despite being "homeless," has "never lost his identity" or "violated the innermost man" (177).

As others have observed, Holgrave bears the characteristics of the propertyless, "self-dependent" young men of the mid–nineteenth century.[38] Proud of his humble origins and full of faith in "man's brightening destiny" and his own "inward strength" (180), Holgrave joins firmness of character to "personal ambition" and generosity of spirit, radical philosophy to "practical experience," "faith" to "infidelity" (181). Restless and unsettled, he is nothing if not another promising young man like Gerty's Willie. "In a country where everything is free to the hand that can grasp it," "the world's prizes" are, if not assured, at least "within his reach" (181).

But if Holgrave is a version of the hardworking and upright Willie Sullivans of domestic fiction, as Phoebe is a version of Gerty, he is nonetheless a far more ambiguous figure. Whereas Willie straightforwardly strives to recover the social and economic position his family has lost with the death of his father, Holgrave, by contrast, admits no ambition but that of the social reformer. Associating with Fourierists, "community-men and come outers," and "cross-looking philanthropists," he gives speeches "full of wild and disorganizing matter" (84). An "enthusiast," as the narrator insists young men should be, his energies are directed not toward individual success but toward ushering in a "golden era," an end to the "old, bad way," the "lifeless institutions" of the "rotten Past" (179). Like other of Hawthorne's young men, Holgrave reveals in his radical reformism a naive rejection of history, a desire to free the present from the domination of the past, to make everything anew. In the context of *Seven Gables* this impulse makes a particular kind of sense, for as the last descendant of Matthew Maule, Holgrave is the product of a history of exploitation, of a slow decline into obscurity. But the desire to erase the past is in him inextricably and paradoxically bound to a desire to avenge it; the impulse toward utopian reform is compromised by the impulse toward revenge.

Thus Holgrave's repudiation of the house of the seven gables as the quint-essential expression of an "odious and abominable Past" (184) and his decision to reside in it represent not simple perversity, as Phoebe suspects, but the contradiction at the heart of his radicalism—a contradiction like-wise inscribed in his change of name, undertaken either to free himself of the burden of the Maule-Pyncheon history or to facilitate his tenancy in the house of the seven gables. Haunting the House of Pyncheon, Holgrave plays the role history has bequeathed him even as he calls for an end to the domination of the present by the past.

In the narrow world of *The House of the Seven Gables*, the historical conflict between rich and poor devolves into the conflict between Pyn-cheon and Maule; the persistence of social inequality is disguised as the ongoing consequence of individual crime. Thus Holgrave's laudable ambi-tion for social justice, shaped though it presumably is by his class history, cannot be disentangled from the desire for private revenge that is the leg-acy of his family history. His passionate argument against the permanence of houses, dynastic and otherwise, is at once a broad argument against inherited wealth and status and an argument against the Pyncheons' par-ticular claim to what he legitimately regards as his own inheritance.

Holgrave's unarticulated quarrel with Jaffrey, the heir to the Pyncheon fortune whose daguerreotype he carries, privatizes the problem of social justice and allows for its resolution through the figure of the model woman. In lieu of the class conflict that binds men together, the romance's ending offers the heterosexual union of Maule and Pyncheon, the in-terclass marriage of Phoebe, who is "no Pyncheon," and Holgrave, who is equally no Maule. Holgrave's restless reformism, his "oscillation," is checked by her "poise," and his world is renovated not by social revolu-tion but by love. Joining Phoebe on her "quiet path," Holgrave trades his utopian dreams for domestic bliss and, of course, in this way achieves them too, at least for himself. The answer to the crimes of history encoded in the decrepit house of the seven gables lies in the prospect of home. Understood in this way, *The House of the Seven Gables*, like *The Lamp-lighter*, offers home in the better sense—in fact, a home where changes never come, built of stone and conforming to the "peaceful practice of society" (307)—as the site of the harmonious resolution of class differ-ence through gender.

But if the conclusion of *The Lamplighter* leaves in abeyance the ques-tion of whether harmony lies in the new world of middle-class domesticity or simply in a reprise of the past, the ending of *The House of the Seven Gables* is even more problematic. Seen one way, the final chapter of *The House of the Seven Gables* simply restores justice of a sort: the Maules get their land back, and the Pyncheons recover their deed. The restitution of one and the discovery of the other lay to rest the crimes of the past. With the death of Jaffrey Pyncheon, the "young giant" of the present is no longer "compelled to waste all his strength in carrying about the corpse of the old giant, his grandfather" (182). History, and with it the conflicting interests of class, comes to an end in a new Eden of love, which, however individual and however transitory, is the only adumbration of utopia in a world renewed at best by "patchwork."

But Holgrave does not simply marry his model woman and regain his land: marriage brings him not only the property the Maules have lost but interest on that property. Through Phoebe, Holgrave inherits Maule's homesite and the house of the seven gables as well as Judge Pyncheon's country estate and his fortune. Just as the new Eden of love is illusory, so too, in *The House of the Seven Gables*, is the perfect harmony of home called into question, not only, as Herbert has argued, because the sanctity of the domestic sphere depends in reality on "womanly dispossession and subordination,"[39] but also because the impulse to "plant a family," to found a dynastic house, is not, as it turns out, peculiar to the Pyncheons but to the wealthy. The conservatism that famously attends Holgrave's accession to property—a conservatism that manifests itself not only in his repudiation of radical reform but in his patriarchal desire to "set out trees, to make fences . . . to build a house for another generation" (307)—is, as the "labouring men" suspect, a luxury of class. No longer dispossessed, his promise fulfilled by bequest, Holgrave lays claim to a future in which changes will not come, to a home in the very best sense.

Chapter II

ORPHANED IN AMERICA

Color, Class, and Community

THE PROBLEM of home—of who is "at home" where and who has the right to a "home"—is not merely a private problem, despite the emphasis on individual self-possession in novels like *The Lamplighter* and *The House of the Seven Gables*. Rather, insofar as homes of the better sort are understood to offer assurance of a fundamental harmony of interests at the epicenter of the social order, in the conjugal family, their import is deeply political.[1] Not surprisingly, then, fictions of home and homelessness and the taxonomic difficulties that attend these have particular resonance in midcentury discussions of the rights of citizenship, the right to claim a national "home," as it were, of the better sort.

From 1820 to 1870, at state constitutional conventions across the northern and western United States, the "legal personhood" of women and free blacks was debated—and largely denied—by white male delegates. The issue before these delegates was whether to grant the vote to women, who had, of course, never been enfranchised, and whether to withhold it from free black men, many of whom had never been explicitly disenfranchised. Framed as a straightforward question of whether certain categories of people, given their sex or race, would be extended full citizenship, the debates over suffrage were, as Rowland Berthoff has demonstrated,[2] anything but straightforward, for they necessarily entailed a delineation of the categories in question. Drawing on the whole constellation of language available for the representation of social differences, delegates to these conventions struggled to find in the putatively "natural" categories of gender and race the qualities that would provide the grounds for conferring or denying the rights of citizenship to women and blacks.

Paradoxically, at the same time that novelists like Cummins and Hawthorne turned to gender and race in the effort to install the white middle-class home as the sign and apotheosis of social harmony, thereby setting aside the possibility of class conflict, those offering a political defense of gender- and race-based exclusions from the rights of citizenship relied on class distinctions to clarify the boundaries of femininity and blackness.

The prolonged discussions of the rights of women and African Americans at convention after convention brought class to the surface as essential to the definition not only of "true womanhood" but also of "true blackness." The integrity of these categories was established by reference to differentials of wealth and power, and these contingent social ascriptions, in turn, operated to shore up the categories on the basis of which legal rights were to be dispensed. At the intersections of categories of race, gender, and class, in other words, lay the rhetorical basis for political exclusion.

For the broad purposes of this study, what is most interesting about these debates is the way they record the taxonomic struggles of the white men empowered to decide the political fates of those different from themselves—and on whom it was thus incumbent to define those difference—and the stark account they offer of the urgent substitution of terms of social difference undertaken, as the delegates understood it, in the interest of social harmony and cohesiveness. More immediately, these debates expose the process by which distinctions of class were folded into racial discourse in the free states; in this sense they anticipate a fundamental novelistic problem faced by African American authors like Frank Webb and Harriet Wilson as they attempted to record the lives of free blacks—namely, the problem of finding a representational vocabulary able to capture an alternative vision of home, a home for those without a home in the nation.

In the case of women, the perfect harmony of interests figured in white middle-class domestic arrangements served to justify and explain the denial of political rights. White women were, if anything, too much at home to need the vote. Husbands and wives, in particular, were regarded by the majority of delegates as "*too* homogeneous for women to need to employ the masculine sort of liberty themselves." "Essentially the same with men . . . yet different" (Berthoff, 781), as one Indiana delegate put it, women, their "image and wishes," were, in the striking phrase of a delegate from New York, "daguerreotyped . . . in the heart of every representative" (774). Identical in their interests but distinct in their domestic office, women needed only "to be heard as women," not as voters (781), terms antithetical in meaning. To suggest that the interests of the woman "whose love has sanctified [the] home" might diverge from that of her men was to "subvert the family" (764). The exclusion of women from the privileges of full citizenship was taken to be essential to their identity as women and as whites: as voters, they would be "coarsened" and "unsexed"; as property holders, they would be rendered less white, reduced to "*jewing* bargain-making" creatures no man could love (774).[3] Indeed, the interests of "*real* women," "the thoughtful and delicate women" (761), as a New York delegate argued, merged so perfectly with those of men that these women neither required nor desired independent political expression; ironically, on that merger depended the very meaning of gender difference. So clearly was this the understanding that for women to repudiate that merger, to assert separate political or economic interests, was, willy-nilly, to compromise both their femininity and their whiteness.

At issue here is not, of course, women's domesticity per se or even their dependence, but rather the class position conferred on some women as keepers of white middle-class homes. Thus, despite their frequent appeals to American classlessness, the delegates framed their opposition to woman suffrage not in relation to those "real" women, the genteel wives, sisters, and mothers of middle-class white men like themselves, but rather with reference to women who were not, in their estimation, "real" to begin with: anti-domestic figures like "kitchen maids, prostitutes, and 'the pretty waiter girls' " (Berthoff, 761). By virtue of a femininity already defined through attributes peculiar to white middle-class domesticity, "real" women would—naturally, as it were—refuse suffrage, even were it offered them. "Working" and working-class women, by contrast, whose disabilities of class were understood to compromise their femininity, would, by the same token, seize the opportunity to vote. In a conveniently tautological argument, the working woman, not her middle-class sister, was taken to embody the danger of women's rights. "Coarsened" by her association with labor, alienated from "home," she was already "unsexed" and thus inclined, so the argument went, toward a "masculine sort of liberty"—the exercise of which would, in turn, serve to confirm her unfeminine nature (761).

Necessarily, masculinity was also placed in jeopardy by the prospect of full citizenship for women. In a remarkable flight of fancy, one Massachusetts delegate articulated the fears of an end to gender difference voiced less dramatically by other delegates. Certain that the "unsexing" of white women would unsex white men as well, he imagined men in a post-woman-suffrage world "imitat[ing]" the "delicacy, the rosy cheeks, the ruby lips, bewitching ringlets, sunny smiles, and all the paraphernalia of rouges, pomatums, pantalets and parasols" of their female counterparts. Abandoning productive labor—"the duties of the farm, the workshop, and the sea"—men, unmanned, would retreat to "boudoirs and shady retreats, in order to become softer-fingered, and more delicate" (Berthoff, 773), ardent consumers of clothes and cosmetics. Crucially, the man "unsexed" becomes not just *any* woman—certainly not a kitchen maid—but a "real" woman, a woman "at home" and at leisure, delicate, refined, and idle. Differences of class are simultaneously obscured and made visible in a fusion of femininity and gentility—and, of course, race.

In the debates over suffrage, all "real" women are white. Likewise, all African Americans are men. Yet despite this fundamental difference in the construction of categories, the language of home that grounds the question of women's rights in distinctions of class is, if anything, intensified when it comes to black suffrage. Though deprived of property and the vote, white women nonetheless had an unassailable right to a home in America. By contrast, the free black man was, in the words of one Minnesota delegate, "a stranger among us"; his real home was in Africa, "among his fellows" (Berthoff, 780). Their national homelessness as sure a sign of their degradation as the domestic deficiencies of the prostitute or the kitchen maid, free blacks were vagrants in America. Widely regarded by whites as profligate, servile, and mentally deficient by nature, the free black man was disqualified from citizenship because he manifested the compound social vices of the lower orders. His disenfranchisement followed from his race only insofar as his race signified what was understood to be his inevitable location in class. In one sense, of course, the danger of a free black electorate could be seen as the same that inhered in giving the vote to white "day-labourers" or "poor mechanics": the danger of enfranchising a class of dependents living—and perhaps voting—at the behest of "the rich man who feeds and employs them" (760). Yet clearly this analogy is inadequate, for free African American men were being systematically excluded from full citizenship even as the franchise was being strategically enlarged to include propertyless white men in the period after 1820. Unlike white waged workers, who might, in the fullness of time, rise to positions of independence according to the likes of Francis Bowen, no such future prospect was understood to attend free black men. On the contrary, the delegates' debates write African American men out of the discourse of "promise." A "hungry [horde] of docile men, born to servility" (761), a "posse of shoe blacks" (772), they were doomed by their race to a propertyless dependence. Permanently dependent, like middle-class white women, and as degenerate as his white working-class sisters, homeless and "hungry," the free black man appears in these debates as the very antithesis of the citizen.

Yet the rhetoric of black disenfranchisement cut both ways. For all their insistence on the innate inferiority and natural servility of African Americans as the grounds for their disenfranchisement, it was, paradoxically, the specter of black domination that animated many delegates. To them it seemed obvious that "political amalgamation" would not only encourage sexual amalgamation but would yield not racial parity but the social and economic ascendancy of blacks. Grant black men the vote, warned one Pennsylvania delegate, and not only will "sable gentlemen," emboldened by their new status, vie for the affection of the white daughters of white men like themselves, but the "sons and daughters" of those same white men will "by and by, become [the] waiters and cooks" of sable gentlemen

(Berthoff, 772). Given a home, the free black man, like his white counter-part, would surely insist upon being master in it.

It is not the arguments themselves that are remarkable here but the degree to which the resort to a vocabulary of class difference in defense of black disenfranchisement could accommodate thoroughly contradictory uses of the discourse of class. African American men were either too de-graded by poverty and dependence to be granted a political home in the United States or they were too aspiring, too aggressive in their pursuit of wealth, power, and social position. Either way—as "servile" political pawns, susceptible to the blandishments or the coercion of an implicitly exploitative upper class, or as genuine competitors for political and eco-nomic power—the black voter threatened the republic and the white mid-dle-class men who were to codify its political future.

The fantasy of black domination articulated by the white men in whom the power to confer citizenship rested and the more widely and violently expressed hostility of northern whites to the aspirations of free blacks frame Frank Webb's 1857 novel about antebellum Philadelphia, *The Garies and Their Friends*. At its center are the social, economic, and politi-cal struggles of African Americans to secure a "home"—not simply to achieve a respectable domesticity, but to hold property, to live unmo-lested, to claim the right to a livelihood, to have a home and to be "at home" in America. Published in London four years after the appearance of William Wells Brown's *Clotel* and long out of print, *The Garies* traces the interlocked fates of two generations of three families—the interracial Garies, the black Ellises, and the white Stevenses—and the impact on them all of a carefully orchestrated racist assault on Philadelphia's black community.

The first novel by an African American to treat mob violence against free blacks in the North or to take up in a sustained way the subject of racial "amalgamation," and the first to find in racial passing a way to formulate the tension between race and class within the African American community, *The Garies* was not a critical success in England despite bear-ing the imprimatur of both Harriet Beecher Stowe and the English anti-slavery activist Lord Brogham. In fact, the limited "natural" literary and moral "capabilities" of African Americans occupied the attention of Brit-ish reviewers almost as thoroughly as their "natural" incapacity for citi-zenship did American politicians. Moreover, the novel's focus on northern racism rather than southern slavery discomfited them.[4] Patronized by Brit-ish reviewers at the time of its original publication, Webb's novel received only scant attention when it was finally published in the United States in 1969[5] after a hundred years in obscurity. Hewing closely to one of two views of the novel, modern literary critics greeted *The Garies* with little enthusiasm. One group of scholars dismissed the novel as a "typical nine-teenth-century melodrama," a sentimental protest novel in the manner of Dickens, Disraeli, Frances Trollope, or, more proximately, Harriet Bee-cher Stowe herself.[6] While applauding Webb's unprecedented account of white-on-black violence in the North, these readers somewhat equivocally located Webb's real accomplishment in his skillful translation into black-face of the conventions of sentimental domestic fiction. On the face of it, this view has its merits. *The Garies*, like other sentimental narratives, suffers from no dearth of melodrama, deathbed repentance, domestic mise-en-scène, long-lost relatives, orphans, and secret plots. Moreover, as is the case in the works of Webb's white and predominantly female counterparts, the problem of finding, making, and keeping a home of the better sort circulates throughout the novel.

But to read *The Garies* as sentimental or melodramatic is, as other critics of the 1970s argued, to dismiss the immediacy of the events on which it centers and to discredit the heightened emotions these events prompt. Defending Webb against the charge of rank sentimentalism, these readers allied *The Garies* with other early efforts at realism, particularly those directed at the plight of industrial workers.[7] And indeed, Webb's detailed account of the politics of anti-black violence in antebellum Phila-delphia is striking for its accurate rendering of a particular urban geogra-phy and its invocation of a specific urban history.

Writing in 1893, the Philadelphia author Charles Godfrey Leland noted incisively that "Whoever shall write a history of Philadelphia from the Thirties to the era of the Fifties will record a popular period of turbulence and outrage so extensive as to now appear almost incredible."[8] The "tur-bulence" to which Leland alluded took myriad forms, from the chronic, local violence of the city's infamous street gangs and fire companies to the dramatic, episodic violence that engulfed whole areas of Philadelphia during the long depression that followed the panic of 1837. "Riotous weavers" and newly arrived Irish workers resisted reductions in their al-ready miserable wages, Protestants crusaded against Catholics, nativists attacked immigrants, and, with frightening regularity, white mobs ran riot through neighborhoods inhabited by free blacks, often with the spe-cific object of destroying black-owned property.

"Hunting the nigs,"[9] as the rioters called it, seems, in fact, to have been a commonplace activity in the City of Brotherly Love. Historians have documented six major anti-black riots in Philadelphia between 1829 and 1849 as well as many smaller mob actions. Not surprisingly, in the same period, the African American population of the city—by 1860, the second largest outside the South—suffered what historian Theodore Hershberg has called "a remarkable deterioration" in their socioeconomic condition. Disenfranchised in 1838,[10] black Philadelphians suffered increased residential segregation, pervasive job discrimination (as well as heightened competition from new European immigrants), and a dramatic decline in per capita wealth and in the ownership of real property in the decades before the Civil War.[11] Although historians diverge in their interpretation of the ultimate—and sometimes even the proximate—causes of anti-black violence in antebellum Philadelphia, as they do over the question of whether that violence was purposeful and highly coordinated,[12] they agree that certain features of anti-black rioting in Philadelphia remained constant. Central among these was the targeting of the homes of "Negroes of property and substance"[13] and the members of Philadelphia's propertied black elite, "men of fortune and gentlemen of leisure."[14]

Read against this "turbulent" history, the interest of *The Garies* lies less in its conformity to the generic conventions of sentimental or realist fiction than in Webb's effort to use these to articulate the peculiarly fraught relationship between home and history[15] produced by racism in rendering the particular situation of free African Americans. As I have already suggested, the literary and cultural representation of home "in the better sense" as a place in which the deficiencies of poverty can be offset by the virtues of femininity, in which social harmony is figured in the perfected relationships of middle-class domesticity, in which model women and promising young men achieve a self-possession that renders them invulnerable to "changes," requires the unassailable, if usually unacknowledged, whiteness of its occupants. In that home, differences of wealth and power are dissipated—and racial differences consolidated—in the language of a gendered ideal shaped at the deepest levels by the ethos of the white middle class yet rhetorically sprung loose from class altogether. Whiteness, that is, is the a priori condition underpinning the possibilities—both literary and social—of domesticity.

Tapping the cultural power of home as the sign of social harmony and the locus of the inviolable private self, Webb, like later generations of African American writers, struggles with its underlying racial subtext. Attending closely to the nature of home for free blacks, Webb reconfigures the problem of black "homelessness." At once sanctuary and stronghold, the black home is, in *The Garies*, the only place in which what Claudia Tate describes as the "Manichean conflict" between "the public performance of . . . essentialized, homogenized blackness" and the "private performance of individual personality"[16] to which racism condemns the black subject can be set aside.[17] Within its walls, the "individual and subjective experience of personal desires"—the narrative of "wanting, wishing, yearning, longing, and striving,"[18] with all its class resonance—finds expression.

But precisely because the black home unwrites race—that is, offers respite from a social universe organized around racial distinctions, thereby challenging the saliency of those distinctions—it is perpetually under siege by those who profit from the maintenance of racial difference. As the central signifier of African American social and economic mobility, black-owned property serves as the lightning rod for racist attack. Unlike the middle-class white home, closed to the public gaze and impervious to change, or the white working-class tenement, with its doors open to the moral contagions of the street, the black home in *The Garies* is always a potential battleground as well as a haven, a "fortress" from which the defense of the right of African Americans to a home, literal and symbolic, domestic and political, must be launched. In fact, resistance to white incursions into the black home stands, in *The Garies*, as a central demonstration of self-possession—a literary enactment of black enfranchisement—even as it transforms the putatively private and harmonious space of home into the site of the historical struggle for racial justice. As Webb makes clear, in a civil polity in which blackness is understood to preclude self-possession, the black home must function simultaneously as the private space in which African Americans lay claim to themselves and, in Robert Reid-Pharr's words, as "ground zero" in the struggle for liberation.[19] The explicit racializing of home thus expands its meaning to encompass not only the domestic precinct in which individuals are shown to elude, however briefly, the homogenized, essentialized blackness to which they are assimilated in the public arena but also the larger community bounded by race, the community of "friends." In *The Garies*, to be without such a home is catastrophic.

The history of such a community of "friends" and their homes structures the thicket of plots that make up Webb's novel. From the moment we meet the Garies of the title, gathered around a tea table laden with chased silver and "all of those delicacies"—from "plump red" strawberries to brandied peaches, cakes, and "geeche limes"—"regarded as . . . necessaries of life" (1) on a flourishing Georgia plantation, the problem of securing a home is before us. The epitome of the rich and easygoing southern planter, Clarence Garie leads a contented life with the beautiful mulatto woman he has purchased in the Savannah slave market and their two children. Legally a slave but, by dint of the assiduous education provided by her master/husband, in every other respect a lady, Emily Garie, as she is denominated, supervises a "fine establishment" supported by a domestic staff of loyal and affectionate slaves who treat her as their mistress. But as we quickly learn, all is not well in this southern Eden. Not only is the cultured Emily painfully excluded by her race from the female companionship of the "white ladies of the neighborhood," but she is similarly deprived by distance of the company of her few "cultivated coloured acquaintances" (57). Without friends, Emily is also and more importantly without legal protection. Nominally Garie's wife but actually his slave, she is barred by Georgia's anti-miscegenation laws from marrying her "husband" and thus legitimizing their relationship and their children; state laws forbidding the manumission of slaves, moreover, prevent Garie from legally emancipating his family. Suffering from both the injustices attendant on her race and the desires instilled in her by the class into which she has been catapulted by her "marriage," Emily persuades her husband to abandon the luxury of plantation life. Declaring her willingness to trade her "gilded chains" (57) for the "meanest living" in the North—an exchange which his wealth fortunately makes unnecessary— she longs for marriage, freedom, and friends in a home in which she imagines character to outweigh color.

This beginning—the Garies' decision to remove to the North—sets in motion the plot, and the plotting, that will culminate in their murder during a racist attack on Philadelphia's black householders. Likewise, it establishes the centrality of "friends," that is, the alliances within and across the divisions of class that organize the homes in which the action of the novel largely takes place. What Emily Garie wants is precisely what no combination of resources and refinement, money and modesty, can secure for her in the world of *The Garies*: the harmonious, racially unmarked home safe from incursions from without and permitting within the unimpeded expression of the private aspirations of its occupants—the rightful home, in short, of the wife of her white husband. Not that she wants to renounce her blackness, but for her, as for many of the mulatto characters in Webb's novel, racial affiliation is profoundly complicated by ambiguities of color. Invariably able to pass for white, these characters must choose to "be" black. They must choose, that is, the benefits of racial community and freedom from fear of exposure in full knowledge of the severe public liabilities to which that choice exposes them. Only by doing so can they, in Webb's fictional universe, lay claim to a home, an act invested with broad political significance.

But in Emily Garie, racial admixture is made manifest as racial ambiguity, her already compromised racial status complicated further by her willing alliance with her white master. For all Emily's longing for a home, the effect of interracial marriage is to doom her to homelessness. Unable to choose blackness without choosing against her husband and their children, in whom "no trace whatever of African origin" is apparent (2), she instead reposes her hopes in the fantasy of a northern home in which class is sprung free of race rather than subsumed by it. Once free, she imagines that her modest, retiring nature, her refined sensibility, her education, and the "goodness of her heart" (2) will win her a place in the society of her peers.

The problem is, of course, who constitutes her peers. As others have observed, the Ellises, whose history intersects that of the Garies, are their mirror image. Servants, not masters; poor, not rich; "purely" black, not "mixed," even their tea—served from china, not silver, and accompanied by corn-cake, not brandied peaches—marks the distinction between the two families. In sharp contrast to the Garies' leisurely existence, the lives of the ex-slave Charles Ellis and his wife, a carpenter and a seamstress by occupation, are devoted to the ceaseless labor necessary to maintain their position as upstanding members of Philadelphia's black "middle class."[20] A "highly respectable and industrious family" (16), the Ellises lend their support to lecture society, church, library, and lodge and hope only to settle their promising son, Charlie, in a trade and their two daughters in marriage. They are, moreover, the proud owners of a home, "bought and paid for" (49).

Unlike the Garies' Georgia plantation that, for all its chased silver and brandied peaches, cannot protect Emily and her children from the slave traders, the Ellises' modest home, with its spotless "little parlor" (45), its "shining copper tea kettle" (17), and its cozy domestic circle, seems, by virtue of its outward conformity to the norms of white middle-class domesticity, a safer place. Conjuring up as it does the inviolability of the private precinct of home familiar from white domestic fiction, that conformity is essential to establishing the Ellises' respectability, but it cannot offer a defense against racist violence. On the contrary, as we discover, what defense there is lies in what W.E.B. DuBois describes as the "community of blood and color prejudice."[21] It is not, then, the respectability of the black home alone but, ironically, its uncompromised blackness that offers safety. While nourishing the individuality of its inhabitants, the black home provides, crucially, clear racial identity in a world divided along racial lines and, insofar as it does so, stands in for the political "home" that is the black community.

DuBois's "middle class of workers"—artisans, laborers, and servants—of which the Ellises are representative constitutes the core of an African American community within which differences of class are overridden by racial solidarity, as the Ellises' friendships with the ragged Kinch and the wealthy Mr. Walters suggest. But insofar as class differences are dissipated by racial identification, the Garies cannot benefit from the interclass character of the black community. Instead, racial "amalgamation" obstructs the search for home as effectively in the North as it does in the South, only in different ways. In Philadelphia, Clarence Garie's whiteness and his wealth turn out to be less important to other whites than the color of his wife's skin—ministers refuse to officiate at the Garies' wedding, their children are turned out of school, and their home is marked for attack by the white mob—while among blacks his color institutes a reserve, a distance, that can never be quite overcome. Having no race, as it were, the Garies can find no home.

Yet even as class differences are overridden by racial solidarity in *The Garies*, different racial affiliations are expressed through distinctions of class. The distance between the interracial Garies and the all-black Ellises is reiterated in the display of class difference, a difference which, given the operation of race, cannot be adequately captured by the distinction between southern landed gentry and northern artisan. Although the connection between Emily Garie and Ellen Ellis extends back to the time of their common enslavement in Georgia, they are unable to sustain that connection, founded in "blood and color prejudice," in the free North, where their different class positions, the mirror and the product of different racial choices, create a social gulf between them. Cleaning and furnishing the comfortable townhouse leased to the Garies by the wealthy black entrepreneur Mr. Walters, the benefactor of the African American community, Ellen Ellis and her daughters express their affection for the newcomers in the manner of servants. The domestic services willingly rendered by the Ellis women—shopping, scrubbing, and polishing—against the arrival of the Garies in Philadelphia simultaneously enact a kind of friendship and uneasily, for the modern reader at least, recapitulate their lives in domestic service to whites.

That the Ellises own their home while the Garies rent theirs is no incidental fact, for the meanings captured by "home" in *The Garies*—from the private space in which a transitory freedom from the impositions of racism is possible to the imagined community constituted by "blood and color prejudice" to the site of resistance to white attack—are consolidated in real property. The Ellises' claim to home, in all these senses, is secured by ownership, even as the Garies' is subject to all the vagaries of tenancy. It is likewise no accident that the ubiquitous Mr. Walters is "a dealer in real estate," the owner of "one hundred brick houses" (50)—including the one occupied by the Garies. Walters typifies the "Negro of property" especially resented by racist whites. Occupying a "stately house," richly equipped with "elegantly carved furniture," French bijoux, and "paintings from the hands of well-known foreign and native artists" (121)—the most highly prized of which is a rare portrait of the Haitian revolutionary Toussaint L'Ouverture in full military regalia—Walters oversees the interests of Philadelphia's black community. His commanding presence, cultivated tastes, and substantial holdings establish him as the equal in wealth of Clarence Garie and garner him, in equal proportions, the deep respect of the hardworking Ellises and the profound hostility of Philadelphia's white political establishment. "As black as a man may conveniently be" (50), Walters is rich enough to buy the hotel that refuses him service and powerful enough to demand an audience with Philadelphia's mayor when anti-black violence threatens. This anomalous combination of color and clout makes Walters a particular target for the mob of Irish workmen instructed by the architect of the riot to render the "lower part of the city" unsafe, thereby driving down the value of black-owned property and forcing its sale at "very reduced prices" (166) to white real estate interests. But that same combination of race loyalty and economic power allows Walters, on learning that the police will do nothing to protect his property, to transform his home into a "fortress" (203) during the riot that derails the lives of the families on whom the novel focuses. Barring his doors, shuttering his windows, and gathering his black neighbors— including the Ellises but, significantly, not the Garies—within, Walters organizes the armed defense of his home against the attacking white mob.[22]

Not every black home can be transformed into the locus of collective resistance to white racism, however. The home of the Ellises, we are told, is "indefensible," not simply because, more modest in construction, it presumably lacks the physical features—the shutters and bars—that enable the metamorphosis of Walters's home into a "fortress" but because it is "situated in a neighborhood swarming with the class of which the mob was composed" (204). Sharing the "lower part of the city" with the white immigrant working-class men with whom they, likewise, vie for employment, the Ellises are marked for white violence by their race, but their class ensures their vulnerability.

But if black homes are not all equally defensible, Walters's house nonetheless stands as the black home writ large. Its defense is undertaken by a motley collection of men of every class—from Walters himself to the notoriously ragged Kinch, son of an old-clothes dealer—and by women. Both Caddy Ellis, who, in keeping with her altogether domestic nature, turns scalding water and cayenne pepper into a weapon, and Esther Ellis, whose anger at the sight of such blatant injustice "takes all the woman out of [her] bosom" (205), play essential roles in the action. This democratic mix of rich and poor, men and women, is crucial to the design of Webb's novel. The battle scene makes material the community of "friends" united by "blood and color prejudice" and, likewise, makes real the possibility of black self-defense—and therefore, self-possession—as, under Walters's leadership, the white mob is successfully repelled with bullets, stones, and boiling water. In the course of the battle, the commanding Mr. Walters is recast as something like a military commander, a descendant of the Haitian liberator he so admires. Appropriately, his future wife, Esther Ellis, not only takes up arms but single-handedly prevents the accidental ignition of the gunpowder stashed in Walter's drawing room, thus proving herself a worthy namesake of the biblical Queen Esther, the savior of her people.

The transformation of Walters's home into a "fortress," the place in which the community founded in race is made material, also (and perhaps not surprisingly) allows a single space to absorb all the senses of home—in fact, all homes. After the riot, the only house left standing of the ones we know is Walters's: the Ellises' home is reduced to "a heap of smoking ruins" (231), its patriarch destroyed both in body and mind; the Garies are murdered, their home ransacked, and their children disinherited. Already established as the site of community defense, Walters's residence becomes, quite literally, a communal home when he insists on taking in both the orphaned Garie children and the homeless Ellises. With Walters's marriage to Esther Ellis and, later, the marriages of Emily Garie to Charlie Ellis and of Caddy Ellis to Kinch—all of which take place in Walters's house—that home becomes a version of the harmonious, interclass black community on which liberation from oppression depends.

Like L'Ouverture the representative of "a small privileged caste,"[23], Walters plays an instrumental role in the black community, a role quite clearly tied to his position at the upper end of the social spectrum. A "race man," he is also a vehement advocate of black entrepreneurship, a man who believes that "The boy that learns to sell matches soon learns to sell other things; he learns to make bargains; he becomes a small trader, then a merchant, then a millionaire" (63). Even the boy disadvantaged by race has promise, Walters insists, and can, with confidence and a little capital, rise. What is more, the systematic pursuit of self-interest on the part of that promising boy will yield the common good, the elevation of his people. Indeed, Walters's own economic and political investments simultaneously generate private profit and benefit his people, just as the defense of his home both saves his elegant house from ruin and rescues his people from defeat at the hands of the mob. In Walters, then, racial pride and a fundamental "American" belief in the promise of unchecked mobility paradoxically—and frighteningly to the whites in power—go hand in hand. Or perhaps not so paradoxically, since in Walters, as Webb points out, are conjoined the "wooly hair" and the "jet black" complexion of the African and "aquiline" features "the very reverse of African in their shape" (122)—the "reverse of African," but not explicitly white. Walter's "singular" appearance indicates his equally singular status within the African American community, functioning as a bodily inscription of his membership in a small propertied elite. But it also serves to establish that the cost of "amalgamation," of African Americanness, need not be the loss of home. On the contrary, racial affiliation is a conscious political act; home belongs to those who know their "friends."

Despite the presence of figures like Walters, class is overridden by race in the view of whites in *The Garies:* assigned an essentialized, homogenized blackness regardless of wealth or power, all African Americans are, as it were, tarred with the same brush. But as Webb makes clear, class must also be overridden by race in the view of African Americans if the black community—the community of "friends" indissolubly bound together by "blood and color prejudice"—is to undertake its own liberation from oppression. The association of ambiguous racial heritage with wealth and status in Walters is thus highlighted and problematized by the range of Webb's characters. In fact, the elaboration of plot and the Dickensian proliferation of characters in *The Garies*, sometimes dismissed merely as an effect of sentimentalism, together assert the density and variety of African American lives. Countering the racist essentializing of blackness that makes the psychological, social, and economic struggle for black self-possession necessary, that assertion is crucial to the politics of Webb's novel.

The character who stands at the furthest extreme of the social spectrum from Walters is Charlie Ellis's friend Kinch. The son of an old-clothes dealer, Kinch first appears as the Topsy of Webb's novel, ragged, undisciplined, mischievous, full of high jinks and one-liners—and decidedly black. Not only does he have black eyes, a "ruddy brown" complexion, and glistening teeth, but his nose, the narrator tells us, is "so small and flat that it would have been . . . a physical impossibility to have pulled it" (29). Kinch, in fact, bears a disturbing resemblance to the "darky" of blackface minstrelsy, as Robert Bone has observed.[24] Even his name— Kinch DeYounge, an "aristocratic cognomen" entirely at odds with his social status—is reminiscent of the ostentatious names assumed by blackface minstrels for their inappositeness. Though Kinch lacks the broad dialect characteristic of the blackface minstrel, his name echoes the malapropisms and mispronunciations of minstrel performance.

Kinch stands in striking contrast to Charlie Ellis, who, despite a lamentable fondness for marbles, manifests all the virtues of his respectable family. Charlie is a promising boy if ever there was one, and his apparently natural abhorrence of servitude and his more specific aversion to livery— the uniform of servility—signal his success from the start. In the course of the novel, Charlie matures from a "bright-faced, pretty boy, clever at his lessons" (17) into a "thoughtful and commanding" young man, kind, good-humored, and successful. Through him, Emily Garie finds her home in the black community, the marriage of her "whiteness" to his promise, like the "marriage" of black skin and aquiline features in Walters, predicting their successful rise. Kinch, by contrast, grows from minstrelsy to dandyhood, from an unkempt boy in a torn cap, patched clothing, and "decaying" shoes to an overdressed clotheshorse whose "blue coat [is] brazen with buttons, and . . . white cravat tied with choking exactness; spotless vest, black pants, and such patent leathers as you could have seen your face in with ease" (374). Yet despite Webb's attention to the difference in their status, Kinch, as much as Charlie Ellis, is a member of the community of "friends." By the end of the novel, he is, in fact, a prospective member of the very same family, betrothed to the "indefatigable housewife," Caddy Ellis.

If Kinch and Charlie Ellis mark a continuum from flamboyance to restrained good taste—a continuum that, in Webb's hands, records social status, not character, and that employs highly conventionalized class markers—the young Clarence Garie lives out the tragedy of the mulatto in whom racial identity is confounded. With the death of the mother who made their mixed blood legible, Clarence and Emily, in whom "no trace . . . of African origin" is visible, must choose their racial affiliation. Honoring "the claims of early friendship," Emily casts her lot with the inhabitants of the Walters's household, "those who have endeared themselves . . . by long years of care" (335). Clarence's tragedy originates in his early separation from those same "friends." Taken from his sister by well-meaning guardians and educated as if white in an all-white boarding school, Clarence grows up longing to take his place in the fashionable white world of his schoolmates. His "education, habits, and ideas" formed largely by whites, he finds the "ways" of black people "strange and irksome" (332) and the "degradations" to which they are subjected an intolerable prospect. Unable to be "white and coloured at the same time" (323), he sacrifices both his sister's affection and the memory of his adored mother to a vision of his future as the "strikingly handsome" husband of the "strikingly fair" Birdie. Responding at once to the lessons of his guardians, the injustice of his society, and the desires of the self, he suppresses his history and passes for white.

Not surprisingly, Clarence's decision is condemned in the novel's most explicitly political language. Accusing him of sacrificing family to self, of trading "friendship" for the "glittering lights" of fashion and the good of the race for social advantage, Emily responds with indignation to Clarence's demand that she forgo her marriage to Charlie Ellis and join him in duplicity. "You," she writes to her brother, "walk on the side of the oppressor—I, thank God, am with the oppressed" (336). As Emily intimates and Clarence himself suspects, he is doomed to suffer for his "false position," as indeed he does. Afflicted with both moral weakness and a physical frailty that serves as its bodily emblem, he lives in terror of exposure, unable to "confess" his blackness to the white woman he loves. As we know it must eventually be, the "secret of his birth"—the "desperate secret" that "like a vampire, suck[s] away, drop by drop, happiness and peace" (345)—is revealed at last by the son of his father's archenemy, the young George Stevens. Having denied his past, Clarence is, in an instant, deprived of his future. Losing Birdie, with and without whom he cannot live, and losing as well the "society in which he had long been accustomed to move" (380), Clarence returns to Walters's house, where, equally unable to move forward to make a home in the white world with Birdie or to reclaim the home he has repudiated, he dies of homelessness. Having chosen to "walk with the oppressor," he ends a "poor victim" of the very oppression he both sought to elude and helped to maintain.[25]

The direction of the black community rests with "men of property" like Walters, whose physical "singularity" signals their elite status; its liability lies, on the one hand, in the propensity of the Kinches to inadvertently exacerbate racial stereotypes by appearing to enact them, and on the other, in the temptation of light-skinned, well-educated blacks to join forces with the oppressor. The survival of the community of "friends," however, rests with respectable middle-class families like the Ellises, who not only found families, buy houses, and "man" the barricades but who consolidate the racial community by marrying both up and down the social scale, both Walterses and Garies, and Kinches. As the language of home predicts, or even dictates, however, the putatively interclass racial community thus constituted requires the universal assimilation to an Ellis-like respectability of all of Webb's black characters. The variation across class and character Webb is at such pains to elaborate must, finally, be restrained, just as Kinch must yield to Charlie's demand that he present a "decent" appearance, "more like a gentleman" (295). So fixed is the association of middle-classness with social virtue that Webb cannot permit class its full range without forfeiting his novel's argument for racial equity. Struggling simultaneously to legitimize black aspiration, to counter racist essentializing, to represent black subjectivity, and to argue for black political solidarity, Webb rejects the sham world of fashion and the desperate world of poverty to valorize an extended racial "family" committed, on the one hand, to a middle-class ethos of honesty, sincerity, individual advancement, and self-possession, and on the other, to the political battle against oppression.

To date, literary critical discussions of *The Garies* have focused on the Garies and the Ellises and, more particularly, on the ways in which these families play out the range of possible fates available to free blacks in racist America. This attention to the contrast between the Garies and the Ellises, between the "amalgamated" family and the black one, has, however, tended to mask a second, and equally important, contrast in the novel between the Garies and the family of the unimpeachably white and thoroughly racist George Stevens. No less than those of the Garies and the Ellises, the lives of the Garies and the Stevens are intertwined in complicated ways by history, blood, marriage, and property. Moreover, just as the histories of the Garies and the Ellises are permanently linked by the mob violence that effectively orphans the second generation of both families, so the futures of the Garies and the Stevenses are bound together by the riot. That violence brings Charlie Ellis face-to-face with the racist workplace that obstructs his efforts to support his mother and sisters and forces the Garie children to confront the ambiguity of their racial position. Masterminded by Stevens, its most direct beneficiary and ultimately its unintended victim, the riot leaves his children too to struggle, albeit in different ways, with the consequences of racial privilege.[26]

Here, as elsewhere in Webb's carefully constructed novel, real estate focuses relationship. The Garies' new home stands immediately next door to that of Stevens, a "Philadelphia lawyer" in every sense. "Slippery George," as he is known, is the "especial friend and protector" of the "swell gentry," despite being considered "anything but an ornament" to his profession by the more fastidious members of the bar (125). Professionally corrupt and personally unscrupulous, Stevens, who orchestrates the white-on-black riot on which the novel centers, serves a powerful white elite whose economic and political interest lies in thwarting the aspirations of the African American community, but his motives are not entirely political ones. Unlike the upstanding Mr. Ellis, who owns his home free and clear, the prosperous but disreputable Stevens occupies a house whose mortgage is held by none other than Mr. Walters, and he is deeply in arrears.

The joint possibility of political and personal gain leads Stevens to organize the attack on Walters, and the same combination of motives inspires him to target the Garies. Stevens's discovery of Emily Garie's race provides him with a handy way to incite to violence the working-class Irishmen who are his pawns,[27] but it is his discovery of his own intimate connection to Clarence Garie—and of the fortune he will inherit upon Garie's death—that drives him to murder. Unbeknownst at first to either family, Stevens is the aristocratic Clarence Garie's northern cousin. He is, moreover, the product of a marriage as "mixed" as that of the Garies. The son of Garie's aunt, a woman long since repudiated by her family, Stevens is the product of the union of a planter's daughter and a "greasy mechanic," a "handsome but vicious" fellow (102).

Stevens is neither a genteel southern aristocrat nor a vulgar mechanic, and his moral "slipperiness" is mirrored in the "slipperiness" of his social status. A vigilante wearing the mantle of the law, a thief and a murderer disguised as an innocent heir, a debtor hiding behind the scrim of a false prosperity, a ruthless opportunist masked by a thin veneer of respectability, Stevens exemplifies the "slipperiness" of social identities, a central concern of *The Garies and Their Friends* and the one that occupies its remarkable middle chapter. In that chapter, Webb demands that we shift our attention away from race and toward class, only to demonstrate the complete imbrication of the two. Using the white Stevens, the product of class "amalgamation," to propound the meanings of "passing"—the subject, in its racialized form, of much of the second half of the novel— Webb brilliantly exposes the disastrous social effects of the pairing of a racist social order with an ideological commitment to individual self-creation. In a putatively fluid social medium in which color is nonetheless taken as a proxy for class and class for character, that ideological commitment is simultaneously sustained and contradicted by the force granted publicly ascribed identity. In a world, that is, in which anyone can purportedly "become" anything, in which yesterday's matchboy is today's millionaire, in which no one can be "known" except by their outward show, social taxonomies of color and class gain enormous weight and have uncontrollable effects.

The pivotal eighteenth of *The Garies'* thirty-six chapters, entitled "Mr. Stevens falls into bad Hands," follows our villain as he travels to the "lower part of the city" at night to instruct the working-class Irishman whom he has blackmailed into terrorizing the prospering African American population. Conspicuous for its incidental value to the plot, this chapter focuses on a sequence of transformations, voluntary and involuntary, in the course of which the effects of the arbitrary ascriptions of class and race are starkly revealed. The first of these transformations takes place at the secondhand clothing shop where Stevens goes to replace his respectable garb with clothing better suited to the rough neighborhood through which he hopes to pass unnoticed. Stevens greets the son of the black proprietor who is tending shop—none other than Kinch—by claiming the right of the white man to name, or misname, the black one: "Well, Snowball . . . do you keep this curiosity-shop?" (183). Stevens's sarcastic greeting intimates his assumption that white men are in control not only of their own identities but the identities of others' as well, but it also forecasts the series of mislabelings to which he will soon find himself subject. Donning a ragged coat in lieu of his usual one, Stevens finds himself thoroughly "Robbed of all appearance of respectability." "The most disagreeable points of his *physique*" are "brought more prominently forward" by the "habiliments" he assumes—these last proving to be "quite in harmony with his villanous [sic] countenance" (187). Stevens's disguise is astonishingly effective—so effective, in fact, that Kinch is "forced to remark" in "wonder" that he "don't look a bit like a gentleman now" (184), and Stevens himself is startled into admitting "how far a suit of clothes goes toward giving one the appearance of a gentleman" (184). Dressed in the dilapidated old coat, Stevens sets out for the tavern in which he hopes to find his agent, the Irishman McCloskey. McCloskey, however, is not to be found.

The formal action of the chapter—Stevens's visit to the clothes dealer and then to Whitticar's tavern—occupies only its first pages. The remainder is devoted to Stevens's repeatedly thwarted and increasingly desperate efforts to return home. This journey requires that he pass through the "lower part" of Philadelphia, the densely populated districts of Southwark and Moyamensing inhabited by free blacks and impoverished immigrants and notorious in the 1840s and 1850s for the violence of its gangs and fire companies.[28] Setting out for home, Stevens is observed by a group of young toughs. As he intended, what they see is not a gentleman lawyer but rather a coat of "peculiar cut and colour . . . rather in the rowdy style" (186). This coat is, of course, meant to make Stevens invisible against the backdrop of urban poverty, but he soon finds himself imperiled by the masquerade he thinks he controls. Unfortunately for Stevens, the coat he has chosen once "bedecked the person of a member of a notorious fire company . . . . the terror of the district in which they roamed" (186). Quite unexpectedly, Stevens finds himself the victim of his disguise. The young toughs, members of a rival fire company, attack him. Too compromised by his appearance to summon the watchman, Stevens tries unsuccessfully to explain his coat and his presence in the neighborhood. His attackers are unmoved and, after beating him, drag him into a wheelwright's shop where they coat his face with tar: " 'Oh, don't he look like a nigger!' said one of the party. . . . 'Rub some on his hands, and then let him go,' suggested another. 'When he gets home I guess he'll surprise his mammy' " (188–89). Home is, of course, precisely where Stevens wants to get, for home is, as the young toughs intimate and as Stevens's adventures confirm, the place where identity is secure.

On the one hand, Stevens's "masquerade" works to perfection: letting the "*appearance* of respectability" drop away, the "disagreeable points of his *physique*"—the trace effects, we are led to imagine, of his working-class paternity—so dominate that the young rowdies easily believe him to be one of their own. Just as Gerty Flint's innate gentility is made material by her possession of her mother's shawl, what seems to be revealed by Stevens's change of clothing is a natural (and naturalized) affiliation with the lower classes, whose representatives recognize his kinship immediately. Hoping to misrepresent himself as a ruffian, Stevens instead reveals himself to be one.

On the other hand, the dramatic success of Stevens's disguise results in a further, and this time involuntary, metamorphosis: Stevens the lowlife is transformed into Stevens the "nigger" as class collapses into race. In a striking acknowledgment of the embattled relationship between working-class whites and free blacks, Stevens's attackers, precisely because they recognize his likeness to themselves, must find a way to mark his status as a despised rival. This they do by changing his color. With his clothes in tatters, his "lips swelled to a size that would have been regarded as large even on the face of a Congo negro," "one eye puffed out," and a "coating of tar" (189), Stevens does indeed, Webb insists, "look like a nigger," and it is in the guise of a "nigger" that he once again starts for home.

But Webb does not stop with the apparent revelation of Stevens's "natural" vulgarity or his convincing transformation into a black. Instead, he carries his account of social masquerade a step further by reversing its terms. Fleeing the backstreets where working-class ruffians hold sway, Stevens sits down on the steps of a "mansion" to recover himself.[29] He believes himself out of reach of his "tormentors" and safely returned to the respectable world he knows, but almost immediately he is beset by another group of young white men, not roughs this time but fashionable, if drunken, gentlemen. Not doubting appearances for a moment, one of the young gentlemen greets him in terms that invert Stevens's greeting to Kinch: "Hallo! here's a darkey!" Afraid that his voice will give him away to the men, some of whom he knows, and that he will have to account for the condition in which they find him, Stevens lends himself to their racist preconceptions by pretending to be dumb. The "well-dressed" young white men first demand that he jump in and out of a hogshead of water, then dance around him, taunting, until one of their number decides to make "a white man of him." "I am going to make him a glorious fellow-citizen and have him run for Congress" (191), he announces gleefully and proceeds to streak Stevens's blackened face with lime, partially restoring its whiteness.

Not surprisingly, this second racial transformation is far less successful than the first. As the rowdies intuit, to make a shabbily dressed white man appear black exploits not only the putative coincidence of poverty and blackness but the powerful symbolism of racist ideology; they believe that the blacked-up Stevens will "surprise his mammy." But the "gleeful" sarcasm of the gentlemen belies any possibility that a ragged and apparently speechless black man will make a persuasive "white man," much less a "glorious fellow-citizen." The ease with which Stevens can be made black is not matched by a similar ease when it comes to being made white. In fact, the final events of the chapter center on the difficulty of reversing the process of blackening.

Left alone at last with a man of his acquaintance—Mr. Morton, a co-conspirator in the upcoming violence—Stevens confides his identity and the purpose of his disguise. So persuasive is his transformation, however, that it is only after touching the tar on Stevens's face that Morton credits his tale. After detailing his adventures to Morton's great amusement, Stevens proceeds once again toward home, his safe passage now guaranteed by the presence of his respectable white friend. "Mr. Stevens falls into bad

Hands" closes with a series of determined efforts to restore Stevens to his "natural" color. First, he and Morton stop at a pump to wash off the tar, but the only effect of their energetic scrubbing is to rub the "infernal stuff" into his skin more thoroughly. When they finally arrive at Stevens's house, his wife, as the ruffians predicted, recoils in fright from his "hideous figure" and "well-blacked face" (192). Once assured of Stevens's identity, however, she promptly undertakes to obliterate the disgraceful signs of his descent into social opprobrium by a cleansing process that literally scrapes the skin off his face.

Stevens can, with difficulty, remove the tar and resume his usual clothing, but he cannot shed his essential villainy. Like the other, more sympathetic masquerader in *The Garies*, the young Clarence, he too is ultimately rendered homeless by his duplicity. Having instigated the riot in order to secure his home financially, by ruining Walters, and socially, by murdering Garie, he is in the end quite literally driven out of it by the fear of exposure—leaping from the window to his death. The illegitimate claim to whiteness, the gnawing secret that destroys Clarence, is anticipated in Stevens's illegitimate claim to wealth, a secret that drives him to suicide. The point is not that "amalgamation," whether of class or race, invariably produces duplicity. Rather, insofar as "amalgamation" enables the misrepresentation of the self formed out of the stuff of race, class, and gender alike, it places both individuals and communities in jeopardy.

Tempting as it is to read "Mr. Stevens falls into bad Hands" as illustrative of the "natural" conjunction of color, class, and character, however, it is precisely this temptation that Webb demands we resist. While the hint of finer feeling anticipates the revelation of Gerty's genteel parentage, Stevens's working-class paternity only appears to provide the key to his corruption. The "truth" of his character, ostensibly revealed by the rowdy jacket and the tar, lies elsewhere. Stevens is not a villain because he is "truly" working class, as the evidence of other, nobler, working-class characters attests, nor is he "truly" black but only blacked-up by white men hoping to prove their superiority. Nor, of course, is blackness "truly" a sign of villainy. Webb's object, here and throughout *The Garies*, is to demonstrate that neither class nor race is a proxy for character—that set of moral qualities understood by midcentury Americans to inhere in the self regardless of social circumstances, class origins, or racial identity.

That is to say, Webb invokes the ideological universe of Maria Cummins and Nathaniel Hawthorne, a universe founded on the proposition that the essential self—whether it is expressed through intimations of refinement and the capacity for housework or through criminal greed—overrides rather than underwrites class and race. But Webb invokes that ideological universe fully aware that the insistence of white Americans on

the independence of character from social circumstance is sharply contradicted by their propensity to ascribe ignorance and degeneracy to the non-
white and the working class. Insisting, then, that Stevens's villainy, while
intrinsic, is not the end result of a genetics of race or class, "Mr. Stevens
falls into bad Hands" offers a brilliant account of the social logic that
allows working-class status and moral corruption to be conjoined under
the sign of blackness to form an associative chain, a syntax of social identity, which, in turn, supports the arbitrary ascription by whites of ignorance, dissolution, and impoverishment to blacks.

It is that logic and the violent social consequences that attend it with
which Webb is concerned. In the course of his masquerade, Stevens not
only finds himself thrust into an alien world of intraclass violence but,
more important for Webb's purposes, discovers, to his dismay but not his
edification, what the black characters in the novel already know too well:
that to have black skin is to be subject to the capricious violence of whites
and is, further, to be rendered "dumb," to be deprived of the possibility
of naming, and thus possessing, oneself.

But if, in a racist society, the appearance of blackness subsumes the
possibility of self-possession, white privilege in turn consists in the enactment of the belief that the self can be so completely possessed that past
and future alike are within the power of the individual to shape.[30] As
Webb presents it, the relationship between these two is complex. Inextricably bound to the promise of mobility, the "privilege" of self-creation
must be claimed by African Americans, despite the disastrous ends of
Clarence and Stevens. As Walters's paean to black entrepreneurship attests, free blacks, disenfranchised as "strangers," demeaned as inferiors,
their aspirations denied, must claim themselves, their promise—and each
other. Only through the energetic pursuit of education, opportunity, and
respectability—the things of the middle class—can they elude racism and
secure a home for themselves in America. Yet that home, for all its cozy
domesticity, does not simply mirror the narrowly ordered, private home
of the white middle class. Its very existence a refutation of white racism,
the respectable black home is charged with historical significance. A refuge from and a defense against the violence of whites, it makes tangible
the political claims of the community of "friends."

. . .

It is instructive to turn briefly from the fictional universe of *The Garies*,
in which "homelessness" in all its forms is experienced most keenly by
men, to the more familiar terrain of Harriet Wilson's 1859 novel, *Our
Nig*, where our attention is directed to the use of race to manage an economic relationship between two women and where home is nowhere to

be found. Like *The Garies*, *Our Nig* focuses on free blacks in the North, but whereas Webb attends most closely to the broad structural ramifications of northern racism, Wilson's narrative draws in painful detail the physical and emotional damage racism inflicts on the individual. This difference—a difference of emphasis, not of kind—is in part accounted for by the change in setting from urban Philadelphia to rural New England and by the change in subject from adult to child. More important, however, Frado's experience, unlike that of the Ellises or the Garies, is the experience of an ever-diminishing world in which death and distance exacerbate the systematic isolation imposed by her mistress. Trapped in the Bellmonts' "Two-Story White House, North,"[31] in all outward respects a home of the better sort, the orphaned Frado suffers from a homelessness that nothing, it seems, can assuage.

The irony of Frado's situation does not escape Wilson. Unlike the white orphans of domestic fiction, whose homeless condition is an accident of fate and whose innate gentility ensures their escape from the toils, both literal and metaphorical, of the tenement to the middle-class home that is their birthright, Frado is introduced into a home of the better sort as a consequence of her orphaned white mother's steady decline in social and economic status. Mag, whose story both introduces and is reiterated by Frado's, is something like Gerty Flint's evil twin. "Early deprived of parental guardianship" (5), alone and "uncared for," she finds not a savior but a seducer. Enticed in equal parts by the "music of love" and the possibility of "elevation" to a life of "ease and plenty" (5), Mag yields to a wealthy "charmer," losing in one fell swoop both the "priceless gem" of her virginity and her already tenuous position in respectable society. But the tale of Mag's seduction and abandonment by the "hateful deceiver" whose voice "sounded far above her" (6) initiates not only the conventional fall from respectability and economic sufficiency of the sentimental heroine but a descent from the condition of whiteness. Living in a "hovel" and supporting herself as an outworker, Mag is unable to compete against the influx of "foreigners who cheapened toil" (8). Losing her "means of subsistence," she is reduced to "drudgery" and, eventually, to marriage to the black Jim, a marriage to which she agrees out of economic necessity alone, even though the kindly Jim brings pity and affection as well as the desire to possess the "prize" (11), the "treasure" (14), of a white wife.

In what might be seen as another exposition on the conflation of color, class, and character like "Mr. Stevens falls into bad Hands," the trajectory of Mag's fall traces a conventional social understanding of the intersection of these three domains. Mag's descent down "the ladder of infamy" into the "evils of amalgamation" (13) ends any "companionship with white people" (15). Yet even when she is stripped of all "longings for a purer heart, a better life" (16), her virtue lost, her "conscience" crushed, and her race compromised, Mag has not reached the nadir of that descent. Left at Jim's death with their two children to support, she is lost finally to "the darkness of perpetual infamy" (16) when she enters a second "marriage" of expediency to another black man, this one without benefit of "the rite of civilization or Christianity" (16). Her sexual decisions governed at every juncture by the hope of economic improvement, however minimal, Mag passes from misery into an "insensibility" (21) that alone seems able to account for her heartless abandonment of her daughter to a life of servitude in the household of the white "she-devil" (17) Mrs. Bellmont.

Inverting the reassuring domestic tale of the orphan's rescue—and the sentimental one of the guilt-stricken death of the good girl seduced and abandoned—produced by white writers of this period,[32] the narrative of Mag's fall into social infamy and her spiritual descent into snarling brutishness tells the story of the quest for a home of the better sort gone wrong. In Mag's story, the orphan girl, left morally, emotionally, and economically vulnerable, is ripe for exploitation by the first "deceiver" who claims to offer love and money in exchange for sexual favors; trading her virtue for social or emotional profit, she is punished by homelessness, poverty, and a publicly damning affiliation with blackness.[33] As in *The Garies*, the conjunction of these, the notion that homelessness, sin, poverty, "insensibility," and blackness are necessary concomitants of one another, comes under scrutiny here. But whereas Webb, as I have suggested, counters the hostile ascriptions of white racism by consolidating the racial, economic, social, and political meanings of the black home, Wilson reveals the systematic production of the homeless "nigger" prompted by the need to rationalize economic exploitation.

Abandoned at the age of six at the prosperous Bellmonts' "large, old fashioned, two-story white house, environed by fruitful acres, and embellished by shrubs and shade trees" (21), Frado is thrust into what turns out to be twelve years of involuntary servitude to a woman whom Wilson characterizes in the novel's preface as "wholly embued with *southern* principles."[34] So abusive a mistress that she "can't keep a girl in the house over a week" (18), Mrs. Bellmont sees in Frado the opportunity to "train up" a servant "in [her] way from a child" (26). Her control of the household largely unchallenged by her well-meaning but ineffectual husband, his sister, and her variously loyal, intimidated, or disgusted adult children, she sets about making herself a slave, a "nig" of her own. But this is not so easily accomplished. The child of white Mag and black Jim, Frado is a "beautiful mulatto, with long, curly black hair, and . . . roguish eyes" (17). "Handsome and bright," she is also, as Mrs. Bellmont's son Jack observes, "not very black" (25).

One way to read the history of Frado's sojourn at the Bellmonts', then, is as the history of the production of blackness, the transformation of Frado into "our nig" that is recorded in the novel's shifts between first and third person. By this I mean not Frado's subjective realization of herself as black and her understanding of the implications of that identity, although *Our Nig* records both that process and Frado's escape from the racist Bellmonts to a larger world in which blackness takes on a more complicated significance. Rather, I am interested here in Wilson's strikingly detailed account of Mrs. Bellmont's project, of her strenuous effort to justify her treatment of Frado by bringing her appearance and behavior, both her performance and her experience of self, into conformity with the terms of "essentialized, homogenized blackness" ascribed by whites to African Americans. Laboring to bring the mixed-race Frado's color, class, and putative character into alignment, Mrs. Bellmont exploits the social logic of racism in her effort to produce the consummate servant: unpaid, servile, and without feeling.[35]

Wilson lays out the stages of this process with remarkable clarity. First, Frado must be freed of any illusions about her status within the Bellmont family. Led through the "nicely furnished rooms" of the Bellmont home, rooms that are "a source of great amazement to the child," she is taken to the suffocating attic in which she will remain for the duration of her servitude. That room—an "unfinished chamber over the kitchen" with a "roof slanting nearly to the floor" and a "small half window" (27), accessible only by passing through a "dark passage" and climbing a ladder—makes material her exclusion from the family and her class position. Pronounced "good enough for a nigger" by Mrs. Bellmont (26), Frado's "chamber" is reminiscent, on the one hand, of the cramped hiding place occupied by Harriet Jacobs in *Incidents in the Life of a Slave Girl*,[36] and on the other, of the dark attic in which the orphaned Gerty is locked by Nan Grant when disobedient.

Housed like a "nigger," Frado must then be subjected to the discipline appropriate to her condition. She is whipped, kicked, beaten, starved, and scalded into compliance with the menial tasks set her; her protests are silenced by force, her mouth propped open with a wooden wedge or stuffed with a towel. But the physical abuse meted out by Mrs. Bellmont in her attempt to bring "our nig" into existence is paired with another, more insidious kind of violence, the transformation of Frado's physical appearance, the destruction of her beauty. Not content with keeping Frado in the "scanty clothing and bared feet" (31) of a servant, Mrs. Bellmont dictates that her color too must be made unambiguously to confirm her lowly status. "Not many shades darker" than the Bellmonts' daughter, Frado is not sufficiently black to avert the "calamity" of a comparison between the two. Determined to "darken the shade which nature had first bestowed upon [Frado] as best befitting," Mrs. Bellmont decrees that "no matter how powerful the heat" Frado may "never [be] permitted to shield her skin from the sun" (39). Dressed in rags and darkened by the sun, Frado must also be shorn of "her glossy ringlets" (68), the sign both of her femininity and, as Jack intimates, of her sexual being. Required to "do the work of a boy" (53) as well as a "girl," both a female child and a servant, Frado is provided no protection by her gender; pain, not sexuality, "delineates her body" and "threatens [her] ruin."[37]

Made "ugly" by conscious design and chronic maltreatment, Frado needs only to believe herself a "nigger" to become one. Here, of course, Mrs. Bellmont fails. Silenced, Frado nonetheless protests; beaten into submission, she remains rebellious; advised to avoid punishment, she instead threatens to withhold her labor; instructed that, being black, she cannot join her beloved James in heaven, she nevertheless persists in her religious strivings. Despite all this, however, Mrs. Bellmont's psychological violence has its effects. Having initially chosen to remain at the Bellmonts' because "she thought she should, by remaining, be in some relation to white people she was never favored with before" (28), Frado is driven to complete her "period of service" (109) not by the fear of Mrs. Bellmont, whom she has "learned how to conquer," but by the fears instilled by her mistress. "Mrs. B. had always represented her as ugly," she muses, "Perhaps every one thought her so. Then no one would take her. She was black, no one would love her" (108). With scant knowledge of the world outside the Bellmonts' "two-story white house," Frado lacks precisely what the free black characters in *The Garies* depend upon, a home, a community of "friends."

Here as elsewhere in *Our Nig*, Frado ascribes her misery to her race.[38] As James reports to Aunt Abby, "Frado's grief, because she is black, amount[s] to agony" (74). And indeed, what Frado naively understands at nine as the affliction of one with "no mother, no home" (46) she comes, under the tutelage of Mrs. Bellmont, to see as the effect of her color: "No one cares for me only to get my work. . . . No mother, father, brother, or sister to care for me . . . —all because I am black!" (76). In fact, as Wilson tells it, it is not the "not very black" Frado's race but her mother's poverty that has doomed her to servitude. And likewise it is not "southern principles" alone but a northerner's keen eye for profit that inspires Mrs. Bellmont's abuse. Doing "the work of two girls," Frado is an invaluable asset, and Mrs. Bellmont is determined to "beat the money out of her" if she "can't get her worth any other way" (90).

Wilson's indictment of racism is the indictment of a system in which class and race are so thoroughly entangled that neither oppressor nor oppressed can separate them. Mrs. Bellmont's economic power is reiterated as racial superiority, just as Frado's ignorance, poverty, dependence, and homelessness are made to seem natural, even to her, by her race. The final, highly condensed chapters of *Our Nig* constitute, among other things, an attempt to separate the matter of race from that of class, to undo the work of Mrs. Bellmont. Leaving the Bellmonts at last, Frado, "black, feeble, and poor" (124), labors to make herself economically self-sufficient, to educate herself, and to find a home. Becoming an outworker, like her mother, in the Massachusetts straw hat industry, she too is seduced and abandoned. Her "charmer" is not, however, a wealthy white cad intent on pleasure but rather a "dark brother" (126), one of the very few "people of color" (126) in her new home. No less a deceiver than Mag's anonymous seducer, Samuel, as Frado discovers after her marriage, is not the fugitive slave he pretends to be, nor does he deserve to be the recipient of her "first feelings of trust and repose on a human arm" (127). First abandoned and then widowed, Frado is, like her mother, left homeless with a child she cannot support. But just as homelessness describes Frado's condition at the Bellmonts', so too it provides the occasion for Wilson's production of the narrative of her life. Acknowledging Frado's tale as her own, Wilson calls upon her "colored brethren" to "rally around [her] a faithful band of supporters and defenders" as she tries the literary "experiment which shall aid [her] in maintaining self and child without extinguishing this feeble life" (Preface). Appealing to her black "brethren" to purchase her account of homelessness and thereby, quite literally, provide her a home, Wilson, like Webb, turns to the community founded in "blood and color prejudice" as her only "friends." Yet the thoroughgoing entanglement of race and class in *Our Nig*, the ambiguity of Frado's color and her status and the inseparability of these, resonates beyond the community of color and frames the communities of interest that stand at the center of the industrial novel.

Chapter III

INDEXICAL PEOPLE

Women, Workers, and the Limits
of Literary Language

D ESPITE growing class segregation, spreading labor unrest, and the increasing visibility of a class of permanent waged workers during and after the Civil War, the influential proponents of the doctrine of the harmony of interests that underwrites the social project of antebellum domestic fiction held their ground. Labor and capital, they insisted, were joined in "partnership" by an "indissoluble bond," their "true interests" made "identical" by the operations of a free market. So complete, in fact, was the identity of capital and labor in the United States, one adherent of this view explained, that the gradations of society "shade off almost imperceptibly" one into the other as free white men move freely between unbounded and largely invisible categories.[1] Specifying only the transitory social location of individuals, in the hands of northern economic thinkers, the language of class fixed neither relationships of production nor the human "types" that some saw as produced out of these relationships. Nor did it, they hoped, differentiate groups whose different life chances might bring them into direct conflict.

But if the doctrine of the harmony of interests of labor and capital that characterized antebellum political theory still dominated the thinking of northern political economists, an alternative understanding—what one historian has called "the heresy of opposed interests"[2]—was nonetheless gaining force. The proponents of harmony exploited a commonplace distinction between free labor and chattel slavery and invoked mobility as the ground for the identification of the independent white worker with capital. They were answered by those who saw not an upwardly mobile laboring class but instead a new form of bondage, not republican independence but the "slavery of wages."[3] The systematic oppression of white workers and the heedless pursuit of profit by those on whom they depended for their livelihood were, as William H. Sylvis, president of the National Trade Unions, put it, harbingers of "irrepressible conflict."[4]

To echo William Seward's ominous prediction of civil strife in the middle of the Civil War, as "heretics" like Sylvis did, was to assert an analogy

between wage slavery and chattel slavery wholly unassimilable to the
"harmony of interests" model offered by political theorists, an analogy
ambivalently received by white workers tutored by republican ideology
to believe that to tolerate slavery "betokened weakness, degradation and
an unfitness for freedom."[5] The more radical of the trade unionists ac-
cused their opponents of ignoring the demands of justice; threatening an
inevitable violent collision of classes, they took to the rhetorical field to
demand both recognition of the dire condition of labor and legislation
to end the enslavement of the industrial worker. Other, more moderate
unionists, no doubt eager to distance themselves from the stigmatizing
implications of the analogy between the black chattel and the white hireling, if not from opposition to slavery in the South, conceded that the
interests of employer and employed might be inextricably connected yet
insisted that the rift between "the class that labors" and "the class that
lives by others' labor"—the "one dividing line" in American society—
was nonetheless unbridgeable.[6]

But if northern white, working-class union men saw violent class confrontation presaged in the divide between labor and capital, so too did
certain northern white, middle-class literary women. Clearly aware of the
metaphors that linked southern slavery with northern industrial dependence, if not of the "frantic denials of those metaphors" by some white
workers, writers like Rebecca Harding Davis and Elizabeth Stuart Phelps
were persuaded that in the absence of amelioration, class conflict would
indeed be "irrepressible." Committed to the unflinching representation of
the desperate plight of the industrial worker, they sought to avert that
conflict by provoking their middle-class readers to action on behalf of a
white working class in thrall to the captains of industry. But in their effort
to render the "heresy of opposed interests" and its attendant dangers in
the emotionally heightened forms of sentimentalism, they fell into literary
"heresy" as well.

Like the domestic realists who preceded them, Davis and Phelps too
sought homes for the homeless. But to them the route to that desirable end
appeared to lie not in the earnest education of the impoverished orphan in
the ways of the middle class but in the reeducation of a possessing class
to which, as they were acutely aware, they themselves belonged. This
difference is crucial not only to their politics but to their art. *The Lamplighter* suggests the social and novelistic benefits of the displacement of
class in favor of gender, of the move from shoes to kittens, for the propa-
gation of a doctrine of harmony. That displacement, in turn, enabled the
white women who largely produced these novels to speak from a position
putatively beyond the play of interests—that is, from inside a middle class
conceived as outside of class altogether—and allowed for the ready assimilation of the orphan girl into the culture of the parlor.

The heresy of industrial fictions like *Life in the Iron Mills* and *The Silent Partner*, by contrast, lies not just in their rendering of a world riven by class but in their narrators' heightened awareness of their own position in that world. This awareness is expressed both by their insistent return to those shoes so early abandoned by Cummins and, as powerfully, by the intrusion of irony into the sentimental literary scheme. Envisioning a social order divided into "millions" and "mills"—those possessed of millions and those doomed to mills (or alternatively, the millions brutalized by industry and the complacent owners of mills)[7]—these writers were pressed to acknowledge their complicity, as members of the possessing class, in the system of oppression they described, even as their peculiar position as women at once excluded them from and exonerated them of responsibility for the economic world. What I mean to suggest is that the project of making the contingency of class starkly visible rendered the disinterested, the "innocent," sentimental narrative impossible. By using Harriet Beecher Stowe's sentimental antislavery novel as a foil to *Life in the Iron Mills* and *The Silent Partner*, I hope to illuminate this literary impasse.

Taking the widening and apparently irremediable disparities of class that marked advancing industrialization as their explicit subject, Davis and Phelps turned from poverty to power, from sincerity to irony. In doing so, they confronted more self-consciously, if not always more successfully, than did antebellum writers the pressure toward the displacement of class that inhered in the literary conventions available to them.

This development can, in part, be seen as an effect of the charged analogy between chattel and wage slavery that hovers behind all manner of public discourse about industrial labor at midcentury, including the literary. Just as the chattel slave—the quintessential figure for dependency of all sorts—shadows the wage slave, so too the sentimental representation of the chattel slave shadows industrial fiction. For Rebecca Harding Davis, a southerner beginning her literary career in 1861, on the eve of the Civil War, surely the most proximate model for a fiction of social reform lay in the wildly successful *Uncle Tom's Cabin*, the work of a woman much like herself.[8] Stowe, after all, had successfully turned the sentimental narrative of the impoverished orphan girl's spiritual and social redemption to explicit political use, pleading for the redemption of a whole "class," as it were, of national "orphans" not from the moral degeneracy of the slums but from the dehumanizing effects of the plantation. Exploiting the conventions of domestic fiction, *Uncle Tom's Cabin* not only racialized the gender-specific plot of novels like *The Lamplighter* or *The Wide, Wide World* but realized in full the imbrication of spiritual and economic self-possession on which these earlier novels traded. To possess the self in

Uncle Tom's Cabin one must, first, own oneself and one's labor, even if
the claim to self-ownership is accomplished by a willful act of disobedi-
ence, the price of which is a martyr's death.

Domestic sentimentalism, that is to say, provided Stowe with the template for an antislavery fiction in which the problem of dependence—for
black slaves as for white orphan girls—could be answered by a perfect
self-control which, in turn, proves to be the route to self-possession. This
is not to argue for the symmetry of white women and blacks in antislavery
discourse, but instead to suggest a representational parity between
Stowe's novel and the sentimental domestic novels that preceded it. Uncle
Tom, in his affiliation with the "feeling" girl, and his proxy, George Harris, the promising young man in blackface, alike suggest how readily the
conventions of these earlier narratives could be transported to a consideration of chattel slavery and, by implication, oppression of all sorts. The
very subtitle of Stowe's novel, with its expansive invocation of the lives
of the "lowly," seems to promise that the economic and political rights
in the self of all those "enslaved" could be addressed and accommodated
by the narrative forms particular to domestic realism. Yet what we see in
Life in the Iron Mills is precisely the failure of those forms to accommodate the apparently intractable issue of white wage slavery.

As I have suggested, my intention in using *Uncle Tom's Cabin* to gloss
Life in the Iron Mills is to elucidate the conditions of that failure. Both
the fluency of Stowe's "innocent" narrator and the plasticity of her black
subject—a plasticity widely reiterated in cultural forms produced by
whites, from the blackface minstrel show to the abolitionist tract—were
enabled by the racial logic of midcentury America. And that logic, in turn,
made possible the sentimental representation of the chattel slave and so
his redemption in art. The contingency of class yielded no such unassailable logic—nor, as I hope to show, could the resort to a racial logic answer
its evils.[9] Putatively free, white, and male,[10] yet hopelessly "enslaved" by
his circumstances, Davis's iron puddler eludes sentimental representation.
Unable to capture her subject in art, the incapacity of art itself becomes
Davis's subject.

Parlors and kitchens abound in *Uncle Tom's Cabin*. Little Eva, arguably the apotheosis of the orphan girl-protagonists who precede her,[11]
moves effortlessly between high and low, white and black, free and slave,
dispensing solace even as her heart breaks under the burden of the knowledge of injustice. And all manner of white people—from the crude northern slave trader notable for his flamboyant dress and vulgar manners,
to the genteel planter with his impeccable taste and earnest wife, to the
respectable Yankee spinster whose consummate self-control ramifies as
perfect domestic order—make their appearances, as do their equally various chattel, from pious Uncle Tom to heroic George Harris, tragic Prue,

embittered Cassy, and irrepressible Topsy. Writing across the divides of race and class with a fluency reserved for the socially and spiritually privi- leged white woman sprung free by her perfect self-possession from the impositions of race and class, Stowe takes possession of her fictional sub- jects with no suspicion of irony.

One of the most popular domestic writers of the mid–nineteenth century distinguished her "primitive" method of storytelling from that of the nov- elist; unlike the latter, she claimed, she simply entered "unceremoniously and unannounced, into people's houses."[12] Just so do we first enter Uncle Tom's cabin. We are invited inside, not by the occupants of the cabin, but by the narrator, who has already taken us on a tour of the plantation house. "Let us enter the dwelling," she suggests, and in we go. While Aunt Chloe tends to the baking, the eye of the narrator pans the cottage, noting its various domestic arrangements and arriving finally at "the hero of our story," Uncle Tom himself, whom we are offered in "daguerreotype": "He was a large, broad-chested, powerfully-made man, of a full glossy black, and a face whose truly African features were characterized by an expres- sion of grave and steady good sense, united with much kindliness and benevolence. There was something about his whole air self-respecting and dignified, yet united with a confiding and humble simplicity."[13] The very fact that Tom is the subject of a portrait, albeit a photographic one, sug- gests, of course, that this is no "thing" but a man. Moreover, the identifi- cation of the portrait as a daguerreotype assures us of its fidelity not merely to the outward man but to the inner one.[14] Equally striking, however, is the narrator's unhesitating ability to read Tom's character in his face. However exotic he may be—with his "truly African features"—Tom is no enigma. His condition as slave neither determines his individual character nor ruins it, as Augustine St. Clare might predict, nor does it obstruct our view of him. He is as confidently drawn as any of the white planters, trad- ers, mothers, or children in *Uncle Tom's Cabin*.

By contrast, when Rebecca Harding Davis introduces us to Hugh Wolfe, the working-class "hero" of *Life in the Iron Mills*, the problem of literary representation and its adequacy arises immediately. The problem is not the story, which is, the narrator insists, a "simple" one. Rather, in sharp contrast to *Uncle Tom's Cabin*, it is when the narrator of *Life in the Iron Mills* sets out to introduce us to her subject that she is beset by difficulty. The narrator's view of the protagonist is obstructed, first, by a failure of vision itself. It is difficult, she observes, to see anything through the stifling smoke of the mills on a rainy day. But she is not only blinded by rain and smoke; her vision is impaired as well by the indistinctness of the object at which she is looking, an indistinctness peculiarly discon- certing when set beside the clarity of Stowe's portrait of Uncle Tom. Yet the reason for this indistinctness is clear. Unlike Stowe's black slaves, white workers appear in the aggregate, as a mass. Although thirty years have elapsed since his death, Wolfe is indistinguishable from the "masses of men, with dull, besotted faces"[15] "creeping" past the narrator's window to the mills in the present of the narrative, "myriads of . . . furnace-tenders" (IM, 14), any of whom might serve equally well as the object of her contemplation. In fact, the narrator herself does not know and, thus, "cannot tell why" she has chosen Wolfe's story from among all the others, for the lives of people like Wolfe are not individual but "like those of their class." Their "duplicates" are "swarming the streets to-day" (15). Davis has no trouble locating Wolfe in history—his own or the town's—or claiming him as a legitimate subject for her narrative. Rather, the problem is in drawing the portrait. Seeing Wolfe as a representative type of the wage slave, the narrator cannot "see" him at all. The problem of representation, that is, is bound up precisely with Wolfe's typicality. Caught in a representational quandary that extends well beyond her story, the narrator is apparently stymied. At once white—in fact, of "a pure, unmixed blood" (15)—and unfree, Davis's iron puddler is neither a promising young man nor yet a tragic one, but only the exemplar of legions of men doomed by the "disease of their class" to "soul-starvation" and "living death" (23). While Uncle Tom can be rendered with all the fidelity of the daguerreotype and, what is more, can be clearly differentiated from the other slave characters in *Uncle Tom's Cabin*, Hugh Wolfe, the type of his class, cannot, apparently, be drawn at all.

Rendering the chattel slave as an altogether American figure of promise, *Uncle Tom's Cabin* provides the theological, the political, and, most crucially, the emotional basis for his emancipation as well as the promise of "another and better day" to come. The chattel slave can not only be daguerreotyped; he can be, as Uncle Tom is, transfigured: by attending to his story, we can move beyond history to the fulfillment of the kingdom of Christ in America—and in Africa as well, where liberated slaves, educated by northern Christians, will "put in practice the lessons they have learned in America" (UTC 626). *Life in the Iron Mills*, too, invokes "the promise of the Dawn," but, unable even to represent its subject, it cannot move beyond it into the golden future. Instead, Davis's wage slave remains mired almost to the point of invisibility in the mud of a present, sinful world. One is forced to ask why Davis's figure of the wage slave resists so thoroughly the sentimental treatment to which the chattel slave all too readily lends himself.

"Stooping all night over boiling cauldrons of metal, laired by day in dens of drunkenness and infamy" (IM, 12), Hugh Wolfe is, by all rights, industry's victim, a martyr of the laboring classes—a Stephen Blackpool or, perhaps, a John Barton. We recognize his story and we anticipate the manner of its telling: the middle-class narrator who invites us to see "the romance" in the daily rounds of the Manchester mill hand or the American slave;[16] the guide who familiarizes the lives of the lowly to the moral benefit of an all-comprehending reader and the social benefit of the oppressed. The tacit understanding between narrator and reader is that the narrator's "lifelike" picture of how the other half lives, a picture both true and immediately apprehensible, will inspire our compassion as it did hers.

In *Life in the Iron Mills*, however, this sympathetic understanding is set aside from the outset. Accustomed to being invited into the story—"Let us enter the dwelling"—by a friendly narrator who resembles no one so much as ourselves, we are instead flatly shut out. "A cloudy day: do you know what that is in a town of iron-works?" (11). The question is not rhetorical but accusatory; clearly, we do *not* know what such a day in such a town "is." "Dilettantes" in clean clothes who think "it an altogether serious thing to be alive" (12–13), we are repeatedly reminded by the narrator that we cannot possibly grasp the drunken jest, the horrible joke, that is the life of the ironworker. We are "another order of being" (27); between us and Wolfe lies "a great gulf never to be passed" (30). Egotists, pantheists, Arminians all, we would rather busy ourselves "making straight paths for [our] feet on the hills" than contemplate the "massed, vile, slimy lives" of people like the Wolfes (14).

Whereas the optimistic sentimental narrative ordinarily projects a sincere and highly impressionable reader from whose eyes the scales will fall upon being confronted with the truth, Davis's hostile narrator doubts even the willingness of her reader to come down into the "nightmare fog" where the millworkers live. This assault on the reader is presumably meant to dislodge us from our position of complacent indifference to the plight of the industrial worker. Self-regard, if nothing else, will lead us to disprove the narrator's charges against us by attending to her protagonist. But ultimately, as I hope to show, the story offers us no alternative position in which to locate ourselves. So blinded are we by the privilege that attends our class and our presumptive race that we are, it would seem, incapable of useful intervention on behalf of the ironworker. And so brutalized is he by the conditions of industrial life that he too is unable to act. Chided into allying ourselves emotionally with the victims of industry, we remain, nonetheless, trapped in our own world.

No sooner, in fact, have we acknowledged both our reluctance and our ignorance and agreed to be instructed by the narrator than we discover that she too is barred from the town. Standing at a window above the street, she can "scarcely see" the "crowd of drunken Irishmen" (IM, 11) idling away their time outside the grocery opposite. From the back window overlooking the river, her view is no better. But here the impediment is less the smoggy day than her own imagination. In childhood, we are told, she fancied a "weary, dumb appeal upon the face of the negro-like river slavishly bearing its burden"; in adulthood, she associates the river with the "slow stream of human life creeping past" (12) on the street. This new "fancy" the narrator quickly repudiates as "an idle one." The river is no "type" of the life of the white waged workers, for its future is assured; it will eventually flow beyond the town into "odorous sunlight . . . air, fields and mountains," while the "future of the Welsh puddler" is "to be stowed away, after his grimy work is done, in a hole in the muddy graveyard" (13).

Brief—even casual—as it is, the association of chattel and wage slave in the figure of the river and the narrator's repudiation of that figure are enormously instructive, acknowledging as they do the failure of "fancy" to suggest even an imaginative solution to the problem of wage slavery. The "odorous sunlight" toward which the river inexorably moves belies its association with the black chattel, bowed under the burden of slavery, whose "dumb appeal" for liberation goes unanswered and unanswerable by its metaphorical connection to the river. At the same time, the tacit linking of the "negro" with the drunken Irishmen and the Welsh puddler recalls the ambiguous racial status of the working-class immigrant. Nonetheless, the contradiction at the heart of the image of the "negro-like river" flowing into an idyllic countryside goes unremarked, while the image is dismissed as naive, merely the product of a sympathetic child's imagination. Associated in the present of the story with the slaves of industry streaming past the narrator's window, however, the analogy fares no better, collapsing immediately into pathetic fallacy. Finally, the narrator makes no use of the potentially charged analogies between chattel and wage slave or between blacks and immigrants. Neither can she sustain the association of human oppression with the "sluggish" river wearied with "the heavy weight of boats and coal-barges" (IM, 13). Instead, her failed attempt to address the "real" in the language of the imagination exposes fancy, the artist's stock-in-trade, not merely as "idle" but as actively misleading.

In fact, the tendency of literary language throughout *Life in the Iron Mills* is to falsify. The mills, for example, in which "crowds of half-clad men, looking like revengeful ghosts in the red light, hurried, throwing masses of glittering fire" (20), are early likened to a "street in Hell," "summat deilish to look at by night," Deb tells us. And, indeed, insofar as the mills are demonic places in which men are held in thrall to the "unsleeping engines" of industry, the comparison is evocative. Later in the story, however, one of the visitors to the ironworks reverts to this analogy, now casting it in the erudite language of the highly educated. "Your works look like Dante's Inferno," the aristocratic Mitchell comments to Kirby, the mill owner's son, "Yonder is Farinata himself in the burning tomb"

(27). The allusion seems at first to have a salutary effect: it prompts Kirby to look "curiously around, as if seeing the faces of his hands for the first time." But if the point of the allusion is to intensify the real, to make us— or Kirby—feel more acutely the plight of the ironworkers, the reference to Dante fails, for Kirby only replies, "They're bad enough, that's true" (27). This response, needless to say, misses the point—as does the association of the ironworker with the sinful Italian nobleman. But what, after all, is the point? The appropriation of the real to the literary is, as Davis's narrator presents it, precisely a way *not* to see. By first casting the mill-worker as Farinata and then by dismissing him as "bad" and thus deserving of such an inferno, the visitors restore the hands to invisibility. The allusion deflects the moral problem that might otherwise be posed by the condition of labor in the mills and allows the visitors to turn their attention to what really matters, the hard facts of industry—"net profits," "coal facilities," "hands employed."

The repudiation, if not the unmasking, of the literary is perfectly in keeping with the dictates of sentimental storytelling of the kind *Uncle Tom's Cabin* represents, with its commitment to the artless, lifelike tale. In a letter to her editor just prior to the publication of the first installment of *Uncle Tom's Cabin*, Stowe outlined her intentions. "My vocation," she explained, "is simply that of a painter, and my object will be to hold up in the most lifelike and graphic manner possible Slavery." "There is," she continued, "no arguing with *pictures*, and everybody is impressed by them, whether they mean to be or not."[17] Stowe's account of her vocation strikes the keynote of sentimental fiction. "Unpretending" stories written to move and instruct the middle-class family cozily gathered around the hearth, these stories were not, their authors insisted, properly "literature"—that deathlike form with "stony eyes, fleshless joints, and ossified heart" fit only for the library shelf.[18]

This is not to say that the sentimentalist denied her invention. Despite her portrayal of herself as a painter who does not paint but only "holds up" the picture of slavery, Stowe explains in the preface to *The Key to Uncle Tom's Cabin* that "In fictitious writing, it is possible to find refuge from the hard and the terrible, by inventing scenes and characters of a more pleasing nature."[19] *Uncle Tom's Cabin* may be "lifelike," but it is not a "work of fact." Quite the contrary: if her critics "call the fiction dreadful," she exclaims in an 1853 letter to the Earl of Shaftesbury, "what will they say of the fact, where I cannot deny, suppress, or color?"[20]

Stowe's two accounts of her role as artist are less contradictory than they first appear. The lifelike tale told by the sentimental storyteller was no invention of a dissembling literary art. It was at once a story waiting to be told and a story everybody already knew—a kind of "found" art. And its claim to sincerity depended on its repudiation of the "literary."

"Literature," in the view of the "scribbling women," substituted artifice for substance, erudition for feeling, author for subject. Sentimental writers embraced instead an ideal of self-effacing simplicity, of "naturalness." What allows Stowe simultaneously to claim artlessness and artistry, then, is a tacit agreement between the sentimental writer and reader that certain artifices will be accepted as "natural," and further, that the "natural" will be understood to point toward the ideal.

In *Life in the Iron Mills*, however, the "simple" sentimental picture is rendered impossible by the inaccessibility of the mills to the middle-class narrator "idly tapping on the window-pane" as if to draw our attention to the barrier that stands between her and the lives of those on the street below. But equally impossible is the self-consciously literary sketch of the kind which Melville, for example, offers in "The Tartarus of Maids," his allegory of female servitude in a Berkshire paper mill.[21] If the first possibility is foreclosed by the narrator's inability to "enter the dwelling" of the ironworker, the second is precluded by her inchoate recognition of the resemblance between economic and literary appropriation. She is no more willing—or able—to allegorize the millworker than she is able to daguerreotype him.

My point is that in *Life in the Iron Mills* we are in epistemological difficulty from the start. The narrator who demands that we "hide [our] disgust, take no heed of [our] clean clothes, and come right down . . . into the thickest of the fog and mud and foul effluvia" (13) remains herself shut in the house. If we could "go into this mill," the narrator observes, we would surely discover there the "terrible tragedy" (23) of the millworker, but this neither she nor we can quite do. The requirement that we enter the mill gives way to a far less strenuous request that we "hear this story." But, of course, we can only hear what the narrator can tell. And just as our narrator can offer only the "outside outlines" of Wolfe's life, so, she claims, she "can paint nothing" of the "reality of soul-starvation" that lurks behind the "besotted faces on the street" (23). Unable imaginatively to project herself into Wolfe's "dwelling," she can paint no "lifelike" picture.

Part of the problem is the ambiguity surrounding that "dwelling" itself. For Davis's millworkers, the central distinctions of middle-class culture are of no consequence. Home is no refuge, and labor is not productive but wasting. The cellar in which Wolfe lives is neither preferable to the mill where he spends most of his time nor, in a broad sense, any less its product than is pig iron. Wolfe's "real" life—as worker and as artist—is led in the ironworks, where, after laboring to transform ore into metal, he struggles in vain to transform industrial waste into art, to render the dregs of industry "beautiful and pure." But if Wolfe's home is "unnatural" by middle-class standards, so are all the other aspects of his life.

Laboring at night and taking such rest as he can during the day, even time is inverted for Wolfe. And importantly, so too is gender: Wolfe's thin muscles, weak nerves, and "meek woman's face" belie his employment as an iron puddler and earn him the sobriquet "Molly Wolfe" among his fellow workers.

Like the feeling Uncle Tom, the feeble Hugh Wolfe is a highly feminized figure—a figure, some have argued, for the female artist[22]—but the resemblance ends there. The feminization of Tom is part of a systematic attempt to invest slaves with piety, innocence, affection, and nobility of purpose, traits meant to assure white middle-class readers of the fundamental ethical and emotional identity, the shared humanity, of blacks and whites. Like Bowen's account of the false antagonism of labor and capital, *Uncle Tom's Cabin* presents the differing interests of slave and slaveholder as impermanent, a chimera of history. Tom's "feminine" qualities are central to his role as harbinger of the social and spiritual millennium to come.

By contrast, the feminization of Hugh Wolfe is both debilitating and distorting. Instead of providing the moral and affective grounds for his emancipation from the mills, Wolfe's feminine qualities ensure his demise. Making apparent his physical and emotional unfitness for the only life he is likely to know, Wolfe's gender deformity, like Deb's physical deformity, serves as a trope for the deformations of industrial capitalism. Paired with the disconcerting strength of the "giant" white korl woman, "her arms flung out in some wild gesture of warning" (IM, 31), whose size and strength are similarly anomalous, the girlish weakness of the feminized Wolfe heightens our sense of the unnaturalness of life in the iron mills and serves, like his sculpture, as a monitory sign of another kind. The masculine korl woman, "muscular" and "coarse," images forth the "working-woman," "the very type of her class" (32). Both in itself and as an expression of Wolfe's inchoate understanding of his condition, the sculpture figures the "soul-starvation" that will, we are persuaded, ultimately lead the "hands" to strike against their oppressors. In his bodily weakness, in his ignorance, in the "morbid, distorted heart" that leads him to theft and suicide, Wolfe himself signals the alternative to revolution, self-destruction. Between these two, there appears to be no middle ground. Neither the platitudes of the liberal Doctor May, one of the visitors to the mill, nor the good intentions of the "Christian reformer," whose words are suited to "another class" (49), nor the wealthy Mitchell's "quiet look of thorough recognition" (39) holds out hope for the future of the iron puddler.

Whereas Davis continually draws our attention to the distortions of industrial life—from the fetid cellar to Deborah's hunched back, from the undersized Wolfe to the oversized korl woman—the logic of *Uncle Tom's Cabin* encourages us instead to see the lives of the slaves as versions of our own. The slave quarters, for example, are as much the outgrowth of a particular system of economic exploitation as the tenements of the millworkers, but Tom's cabin is nonetheless presented to us not as a hovel but as a veritable bastion of domesticity. Only the easy intrusion of whites—slaveholders, slave traders, and narrators—into the cabin reminds us that, for the slave, there is neither privacy nor security at home. In both *Uncle Tom's Cabin* and *Life in the Iron Mills*, the distinctions between the public and the private, between work and family, so scrupulously maintained by the middle class, are compromised, but in one we witness the doomed but insistent efforts of the chattel slave to restore the boundary between these, while in the other the normative arrangements of the middle class are beyond the imagination as well as the capacity of the characters. Unlike Chloe and Tom, neither Wolfe nor Deborah, for all their discontent, sees his or her "betters" as imitable.

Since the narrator of *Life in the Iron Mills* has located her characters in a wholly alien world, it is not surprising that she can offer only the "fragments" of a story, the "outside outlines of a night" (IM, 23). By contrast, the narrator who so unceremoniously enters Uncle Tom's cabin is, so to speak, in full possession of her subject. Uncle Tom, after all, belongs quite literally to whites like herself and her readers. This is not to suggest that Stowe did not mean to extend a full humanity to her slave characters; nevertheless, the central concern of *Uncle Tom's Cabin*—the transformation of a "thing" into a "man"—implies a plasticity that lends itself to Stowe's literary as well as her political purposes even as the form of representation she invokes—the daguerreotype—paradoxically hints at a deathlike fixing of its subject. The literal appropriation of the labor of slaves, in other words, facilitates their literary appropriation by the white artist.

For romantic racialists like Stowe, the untapped potential of blacks provided one of the most pressing arguments against slavery. Like the Swedenborgian Alexander Kinmont, who claimed that blacks were destined to develop "a later but far nobler civilization" than that of whites, or William Ellery Channing, who saw in blacks "the germs of a meek, long-suffering, loving virtue,"[23] Stowe projects a rosy future in which the enslaved black emerges as the free, Christian, and altogether respectable citizen of Liberia. That future is, of course, intimated from the outset by Uncle Tom's cabin, which—from its neat garden patch to the carpeted corner that serves as "drawing room" and the "brilliant scriptural prints" that decorate its walls—resembles nothing so much as the "parlor" Gerty creates for Trueman Flint, a playhouse in which the genteel life of middle-class adulthood is being rehearsed.

The prophetic mode of Stowe's narrative depends, in other words, on the plasticity of its object, the black slave, and that plasticity in turn is a central feature of the developmental schemes used by some white opponents of slavery to understand both the present and the future of the slaves. As yet unmade, the black could be molded to the artist's liking. In fact, he could be cast, as he is in *Uncle Tom's Cabin*, more or less in the image of his white creator.[24] What is reflected here is not the sentimentalist's "ability to confuse the natural and the ideal"[25] so much as her willingness to reimagine the real as a type of the ideal. The success of *Uncle Tom's Cabin* depends on the narrator's capacity to project in fully realized form the individuality of the man who lurks in the "thing" and, on the basis of this projection, to call for his emancipation. Insofar as it draws out the human potential—that is, the potential for feeling—in those whose full humanity is in doubt—the slave or, more commonly, the unruly orphan girl—sentimental narrative is oriented always toward the future[26] and, I would suggest, toward the forms of home, where differentials of class are most conspicuously inscribed.

A "type" not of the ideal but of the actual, Hugh Wolfe, unlike the malleable Uncle Tom, must be "hewed and hacked" out of the recalcitrant korl—the industrial waste that is both his sculptural medium and his matter—by a doubting narrator who questions the capacity of literary language to make his story "a real thing" to her resisting reader. The object of the narrator's regard in *Life in the Iron Mills* is not the man *in posse* but the man the industrial world has already produced, the man with no future. Fixed in an interminable present, inarticulate, uneducated, born "in vice," "starved" in infancy, stained in body and soul, Wolfe is, so to speak, already completed—or, rather, finished.

The irony is obvious, for Hugh Wolfe, unlike Uncle Tom, is free, white, and male. He is not legally bound to the mills; on the contrary, he is, as we say, master of his own destiny. As Doctor May complacently remarks, "you have it in you to be a great sculptor. . . . A man may make himself anything he chooses. . . . Make yourself what you will. It is your right" (IM, 37). A free agent by right, Wolfe is nonetheless pictured as entirely the victim of his circumstances, a figure not of human potential but of human waste.

But he is also, of course, a figure of the artist. The argument for Wolfe's redemption lies not in the man, dumb and brute-like, but in the korl woman, whose "wild, eager face, like that of a starving wolf's" (IM, 32), is, like the starving Hugh Wolfe, incomprehensible to the jeering Kirby and the complacent Doctor May. Nor can Wolfe explain it. Only the coolly detached and thoroughly patrician Mitchell sees "the soul of the thing," but he sees it with an eye "bright and deep and cold as Arctic air," the eye of an "amused spectator at a play" (36). The korl sculpture, the tragedy of the iron puddler, the "rare mosaic" he examined that morning, and, we must assume, the peculiar institution of the South he has come

to the border state to "study"—these are to him as one. The narrator of
Life in the Iron Mills must defend her subject not only against the Kirbys,
who would deny his soul, and the genial Mays, who would deny his
plight, but, most crucially, against the tranquil gaze, the reified consciousness, of the Mitchells, who see in Wolfe an "amusing study"—all of these,
it must be added, versions both of narrator and of reader.

Needless to say, the vehemence of the narrator, her inversion of the
usual narrative stance, her insistence on the failure of the literary, and her
own inadequacy are all calculated for effect. She does, after all, tell her
story and more. For as she herself admits, the "tiresome" story of Hugh
Wolfe hides a "secret" that she "dare not put . . . into words," a "terrible
dumb question" that is, paradoxically, "from the very extremity of its
darkness, the most solemn prophecy . . . the world has known of the Hope
to come" (IM, 14). The question—"Is this the End?"—is articulated only
twice: once in the poetic epigraph that opens the story, and again, at its
close, by the korl woman.

Complicit though art may be in the system of capitalist exploitation,
only art, it turns out, can speak the terrible question and reveal the prophecy. Wolfe is mute, but his sculpture is invested with the power of speech.
The "pale, vague lips" of the korl woman "tremble" with the terrible
question (IM, 64). Wolfe cannot be figured, much less transfigured, but
the korl woman is touched by the "blessing hand" of the "Dawn" (65)
just as Deborah, named after a prophetess, the mother of Israel, is later
"touched" by the Quaker woman.

But prophecy, both social and religious, fails in *Life in the Iron Mills*
because in the end art has been made to substitute for life after all. That
is to say, prophecy fails because the narrator has made us acutely aware
not only of the distance between the artifice (the story or the sculpture)
and the "Truth" (the "reality" of Hugh Wolfe's "soul-starvation") but of
the inevitable tendency of art to appropriate the life of its subject, the mill
hand, just as the mill owner appropriates his labor. Thus, when we learn
of Deborah's transformation at the hands of the Quakers in a "homely
pine house, on one of these hills" overlooking "broad, wooded slopes and
clover-crimsoned meadows" (63), we cannot but realize that we are being
asked to accept the pathetic fallacy of the river after all. Likewise when
the narrator attempts, at the close of the story, to re-present the truth of
Hugh Wolfe's futile life as a higher one, the transcendent truth of "the
day that shall surely come," we read ironic posturing;[27] the narrator has
instructed us too well in the empty rhetoric of sentimental Christianity.
Fully persuaded that the furnace-tender lives and dies in the mills only to
be replaced by his duplicate, that his aspirations will always be thwarted
by the conditions of industrial life, we believe that he is America's future—
he will no more disappear than the wheels of industry will grind to a halt—
but he prefigures not the millennium but, we suspect, the apocalypse.

Insofar as the brutalizing effects of wage slavery are pictured as the necessary concomitant of industry, they appear irremediable and, like the mills themselves, inescapable. Chattel slavery, by contrast, could be abolished—and that without endangering the nation. For Stowe's narrator, slavery is not just a sin but an anachronism and an aberration. Unlike industry, it is the remnant of an altogether un-American seignorialism, belonging to the feudal past, not the democratic future. As George Harris's invocation of the American Revolution implies, slavery constitutes a falling away from the very ideals on which the nation was founded. Emancipation, in *Uncle Tom's Cabin*, does not then threaten but rather guarantees the future of America; in fact, emancipation alone, as Stowe suggests at the close of her novel, will avert the wrath of God and secure America for the millennium. Moreover, emancipation not only must but can be accomplished. Despite the fact that the narrator goes to some lengths in *Uncle Tom's Cabin* to demonstrate the complicity of the North in southern slavery, she understands the effects of emancipation as local and short-term. Once possessed of "property, reputation, and education" and all the advantages of "Christian republican society," the emancipated slaves can be returned to Africa to put in practice "the lessons they have learned in America" (UTC, 449).

If one were to credit their titles alone, to go from *Uncle Tom's Cabin* to *Life in the Iron Mills* is simply to go from home to work. At the imaginative center of Stowe's narrative is the family home, its affectionate ties the story's ideal, its disruption a sin, its absence the sign of an unredeemable evil. Uncle Tom's "real" life is led in his cabin, surrounded by his wife and children. An ideal site, the cabin thus can serve, at the end of the narrative, as a "memorial," pointing simultaneously back to slavery, a death in life, and forward to emancipation, a life after death.

In establishing the affective grounds for the identification of her middle-class reader with the slave, Stowe's narrator invests her black characters with the virtues they will, she assures us, come to have once free. In this sense, Uncle Tom and his fellow slaves fuse hope and destiny. Even more acutely than the middle class of whom it has been claimed, the slaves in *Uncle Tom's Cabin* live "suspended between the facts of [their] present social condition and the promise of [their] future."[28] And just as the middle-class American was thereby plagued with anxiety concerning his own social identity, so too, one might argue, was he plagued with anxiety over the identity of the African American. In that anxiety we can, perhaps, read the demise of slavery. Stowe's "monumental effort to reorganize culture from the woman's point of view"[29] is, I mean to suggest, an effort to reorganize culture from the unselfconscious perspective of the white, middle-class woman for whom the contradictions of sentimental appropriation posed no difficulty.

The drive to impose the forms of the future on the present, so apparent in *Uncle Tom's Cabin*, is stymied in *Life in the Iron Mills*, where all forward movement is blocked by the combination of inadequate narrator, unwilling reader, and mute subject. Importantly, it is not the condition of labor that obstructs the vision of amelioration: even where home is a cellar with a pile of rotting straw for a bed, where "real" life is stooping over a cauldron of boiling metal all night, it is possible to project a future millennium in which masters and men, Christians all, unite. But it is possible only by an act of appropriation. With an irony that eludes its unselfconscious narrator, *Uncle Tom's Cabin* appropriates the black slave—an embodied object, a "thing" waiting to be claimed—in the interest of ending his appropriation by others. This same irony is all too apparent to the narrator of *Life in the Iron Mills*. Rejecting all modes of representation as forms of appropriation, refusing to pretend to know her subject just as she refuses to let her reader pretend to know what a cloudy day in an iron mill town is, she exposes the artless sentimentalists and the erudite literati—Stowe and Melville alike—in their truest character, as members of the possessing class.

Yet like them, Davis must find a way to tell her story. Ostensibly freeing her eyes to see the promise of the "Dawn" in the nearly impenetrable darkness of her story, she falls victim to the common fate of the reforming artist. Having refused to take possession of her human subject, she is, in the end, the uneasy possessor of the korl woman, the only remaining evidence of Wolfe's existence. *Uncle Tom's Cabin* ends with the transfiguration of Tom's homely dwelling into the symbolic site of liberation; *Life in the Iron Mills* ends as it begins. Just as Hugh Wolfe is rendered invisible by the smoke of the mills at the beginning of the story, so at the end, the visible, tangible figure of the korl woman, "a rough, ungainly thing," painful to look at, is kept hidden behind a curtain in the narrator's library with its genteel assemblage of the stuff of the nineteenth-century culture of sincerity: "a half-moulded child's head; Aphrodite; a bough of forest-leaves; music; work; homely fragments, in which lie the secrets of all eternal truth and beauty" (IM, 65). Occasionally, we are told, when "the curtain is accidentally drawn back," the "spirit of the dead korl-cutter looks out" (64) through its "woeful" face and the narrator is recalled to the "terrible question" posed by his fate. But even as that question is putatively answered by the "cool gray light" that "touches its head like a blessing hand," the "desperate need" of the korl woman and its maker remains (65).

For Stowe, slavery is the testing ground of middle-class culture. The success of *Uncle Tom's Cabin* depends on the placement of the chattel slave in a developmental scheme that makes immanent his good character and thus brings him, provisionally at least, into the world of the reader.

The virtues of that world are measured, in turn, by its capacity to assimilate to itself both slave and slaveholder. In other words, the developmental scheme that governs the representation of slaves in *Uncle Tom's Cabin* not only lends itself to the millennial hopes of the narrator but also implies an absolute standard of value against which everyone and everything can be measured.

In Davis's grim account of industrial life, on the contrary, we are returned finally to the domestic world of the middle-class narrator, which, unlike the satanic mills, "belongs to the open sunlight" (IM, 65). But that world—a world in which vision is ostensibly restored—is one in which, not surprisingly, millworkers become once again invisible, a world from which darkness is banished and in which epistemological questions are answered by sentimental piety. Having placed the wage slave out of sight of that world and beyond the ameliorative influence of genteel reform, the narrator is left with only a morally equivocal art to mediate between the sunlit world of her middle-class reader and the gloom of the mills. The effects of class cannot be dismissed as obscuring a deeper "humanity" in the millworker, nor can the vocabularies of race or gender ameliorate those effects. Rather, class stands as irreducible to the end in *Life in the Iron Mills*. And the questionable capacity of art—suspect from the first— to represent, much less redeem, the iron puddler becomes itself the story's subject.

· · ·

To say that *Life in the Iron Mills* fails to redeem its working-class protagonist is emphatically not to say that the story itself was a failure. *Life in the Iron Mills* was accepted for immediate publication in the illustrious *Atlantic Monthly* by James T. Fields, much to the surprise of its then unknown author. Even at Davis's death, nearly sixty years later, it was this depiction of "the grinding life of the working people around her" that the *New York Times* chose to laud in its obituary, citing the "attention" Davis's story attracted "from all over the country." The story so dramatically exploded the sentimental conventions of its day that, as the *Times* noted, its "stern but artistic realism" led "many" to think "the author must be a man," "a man of power not unlike Zola's."[30]

A year after Rebecca Harding Davis's death in 1909 and a year before her own, Elizabeth Stuart Phelps, first famous as the author of the enormously popular *The Gates Ajar* (1868), acknowledged the abiding impact of *Life in the Iron Mills* on her "moral nature" and her intellectual development as a writer. "That story," she explained in an essay entitled "Stories That Stay," "was a distinct crisis for one young writer": "It was never possible after reading it to ignore. One could never say again that one did not understand. The claims of toil and suffering upon ease had assumed a new form. For me they assumed a force which perhaps it is not too much to say, has never let me go."[31] The most immediate evidence of the "claims" made upon the younger author by Davis's story is Phelps's own *The Silent Partner*, published a decade after the appearance of *Life in the Iron Mills*. Like its predecessor, *The Silent Partner* is a novel in which the politics of representation, the formal imperatives of domestic sentimentalism, and the reformist intent of the author stand in radical tension.

Written at a moment when, by almost any measure, Americans' awareness of class divisions was at its most acute,[32] *The Silent Partner* centers on the evolving relationship between Perley Kelso, a pampered mill owner's daughter, and a ragged factory girl named Sip Garth. Following a brief and entirely accidental encounter in Boston, Perley and Sip meet again, three weeks later, in the mill town of Five Falls, to which Perley has repaired after her father's sudden death in an industrial accident. Awakened from the moral and emotional stupor in which she has heretofore subsisted by Sip's appalling account of the conditions in the mill to which she has fallen heir, Perley informs her fiancé, the junior partner in the firm, of her decision to take an active role in the running of the mill. As her father's sole heir, she assumes that the position of partner is hers by right, only to learn that she commands nothing more than "a certain share of interest." Relegated to the position of silent partner, Perley devotes her time to improving the lot of the mill operatives.

The revelation of her powerlessness in the firm, however, pushes Perley to a realization of her larger powerlessness as a woman—a powerlessness mirrored in Sip, the conditions of whose life are dictated by the men who run the mills—and, thence, to a repudiation of marriage, which, even when founded on love, appears to her as yet another silent partnership. Refused a partnership in the mill and rejecting the partnership of marriage, Perley enters into a partnership of another kind with Sip, who likewise rejects her suitor. Their alliance, founded on gender identity and reinforced by their common orphanhood, is characterized by an interdependence in which Sip lends Perley access to the tenements while Perley introduces Sip to the parlor. The partnership that liberates Perley from marriage and enables her benevolent activity on behalf of the working poor likewise gives Sip a voice. Forgoing her early aspirations to the music hall stage, Sip takes her place instead as a street preacher at the end of the novel.

Episodic in its construction, *The Silent Partner* moves the reader through a series of views of the life of labor as Perley learns how the other half lives. The working-class family is revealed in all the dysfunction poverty has produced; the blacklisted trade unionist, the factory operative turned partner, the striking mob, and the heartless mill owner "fil[ing] handcuffs . . . against the day when [his] 'hands' shall have gone hungry long enough"[33] all make their appearance, as do the representatives of an oblivious upper class who profit by the labor of unseen workers.

The mission of *The Silent Partner* is clear: the novel is intended to prompt "intelligent manufacturers" to expend their "Christian ingenuity" to ameliorate the lot of their employees. The origins of Phelps's fiction in the factual is, as it is in *Uncle Tom's Cabin*, crucial to the novel's purpose. "Every alarming sign and every painful statement," we are assured, is attested to by the reports of the Massachusetts Bureau of Statistics of Labor and by eyewitnesses to the conditions in the textile mills. Explicitly the story of an encounter between capital and labor, *The Silent Partner* sets "ease and toil . . . millions and mills" in sharp contrast. Structured by the public debates of the 1870s over the relationship between capital and labor, the "argument" of *The Silent Partner* is familiar. Invoking the unbridgeable gulf between those who labor and those who subsist on the labor of others, Phelps allowed the interdependence of labor and capital but insisted, with trade unionists like William Sylvis, that the two were not therefore "partners in the same concern":[34] one, after all, owned shares in the firm, while the other did not.

Likewise Perley and Sip. *The Silent Partner* begins by directing our attention to the material circumstances that separate Phelps's female representatives of capital and labor. As she does elsewhere in her fiction, Phelps draws these distinctions with devastating class specificity. Perley, "swathed to the brain" in comfort, is introduced on a rainy afternoon sitting in her father's library before a "cannel blaze" contemplating an evening at the opera (SP, 11). Her idleness is matched only by her familiarity. Beautiful, wealthy, indulged, and unconscious, Perley is scarcely in need of "the ceremony of an introduction" (9). She is, it seems, the very type of her class and sex: "twenty-three . . . the daughter of a gentleman manufacturer . . . a resident of Boston" (9), and engaged to marry her father's junior partner. An "indexical" person who never does "anything that is not worth watching," she nonetheless does almost nothing, though she is much observed. She exerts herself only to order her dinner and to choose, with impeccable taste, the scent for her carriage. Despite the "passions of superfluous life" from which she intermittently suffers, Perley is as devoid of mental and emotional activity as she is of physical occupation. Throughout the rainy afternoon, she has "found no occasion to dampen the sole of her delicate sandals" nor "found herself to be the possessor of . . . [a] thought since dinner" (11). Admired for her taste and beauty, Perley is engulfed to the point of drowning in luxury.

Her beringed hands "folded . . . like sheets of rice paper" (13), Perley stands at the greatest possible distance from the mill hand Sip, who is threatened by a deluge of a different kind. While Perley traces the "chromatic run" of the raindrops on her window with idle hands, Sip battles with the storm out on the street. En route to the opera, Perley follows with interest and amusement Sip's "manful struggles" with the wind, as she strikes "out with her hands as a boxer would" and pommels the wind "with her elbows and knees like a desperate prize-fighter" (17). Dressed in a dingy plaid dress, Sip is ragged and bitter and, as Perley discovers when, on a whim, she invites Sip to shelter in her newly scented carriage, smelly. She is also, and importantly, unfeminine.

While rarely acknowledged as figures of class per se, these are nonetheless conventional literary representations. Modeled on the wealthy and self-indulgent belle of antebellum domestic fiction who serves as the foil for the middle-class protagonist, Perley is so familiar that we not only already know her, but we know from the moment of her introduction that we are to condemn her idleness and excess. Likewise, Sip conforms, morally if not physically, to an existing model of the honest working girl in whom the problems of industrial life were distilled for the stage.[35]

Class estrangement is rendered from the start of *The Silent Partner* in a standing vocabulary of gender. That is to say, the distance across which Sip and Perley meet is marked, on one side, by Perley's decorative, genteel femininity and, on the other, by Sip's "manful" struggle. But that vocabulary, deployed to distinguish between millions and mills, functions to a different end in Phelps's novel. Ordinarily, the excesses of the belle of domestic fiction serve to highlight the genteel virtues of the protagonist with whom she is paired, while these same virtues in the honest working girl magically summon the economic resources that will allow for their full expression. At the outset of *The Silent Partner*, however, no such virtuous woman exists, and gender ideologies are deconstructed as an aspect of class. By this I mean not only that gender is expounded as a marker of class difference but that it is offered as the product of class position. Gender ideologies are presented as an intrinsic feature of class.

Forced to struggle "manfully" to earn her keep in a weaving room that pits the dehumanized "hand" against an all-too-human machine that "rage[s] . . . throws its arms about . . . shakes at the elbows and knees . . . writhes and roars" (SP, 76), Sip suffers under the arbitrary impositions of an industrial workplace where conventional distinctions of gender are routinely abrogated. In fact, one of the crimes of capital lies precisely in its willingness to sacrifice gender difference to the goals of production. Sip is dehumanized exactly to the extent that she is masculinized; what the mills take from her is her femininity. Similarly, Perley's highly ornamental and utterly idle femininity—a femininity that leads her suitors to relegate her to the position of a "lay figure"—is equally dehumanizing. Swaddled in luxury, lulled by admiration, she at first neither thinks nor feels, much less acts. Perley's membership in the capitalist class depends on her idle femininity as surely as Sip's identity as wage slave rests on her "masculinity." Having exposed the class origins of gender formations, Phelps can represent Sip's struggles and Perley's indolence as equally unnatural, equally signs of the distorting effects of industrial capitalism.

But the associative chain that defines social identity does not end with gender. Phelps's use of the vocabulary of gender to indicate the distance between Perley and Sip is reiterated in the vocabulary of race. Again and again, the reader's attention is drawn to Sip's "little brown face."[36] She is one of a "great many muddy people" (SP, 17), people whom the sleet does not "wash . . . as fast as the mud splatter[s] them" (17). Accosting Perley at the opera house, with the elegant crowd breaking in "billows about her," Sip is as "black and warning as a hidden reef" (29). Lest we miss the point, Sip, the wage slave, herself expounds her relation to blackness in the course of explaining why she will never marry: "I'll never bring children into this world to be factory children . . . never. I've heard tell of slaves before the war that wouldn't be fathers and mothers of children to be slaves like them. That's the way I feel. . . . I'll never marry anybody" (287–88). Sip, of course, is white, not black, as much a "Yankee" as Perley with her Pilgrim forebears. Since she is employed in the mills, not the fields, there is no natural explanation for her brown skin—in fact, the other weavers in the mill where she works are, we are told, recognizable by their bleached skin—but the historical explanation is not hard to find.

The sign of her enslavement, Sip's dark skin is made explicable by the debate over class harmony. The ideology of free labor obviates class conflict by imputing mobility to the wage laborer; the harmony of class interests is guaranteed, that is, by individual change over time. Conversely, the representation of the wage laborer as chattel fixes the class location of the individual; only social revolution or benevolent intervention on the part of the powerful can alter his condition. Not surprisingly, then, in *The Silent Partner* economic mobility is rendered next to impossible. Even the novel's exemplary man, Stephen Garrick, who has miraculously moved from a life of poverty in the mills to the partnership Perley covets, insists that his economic rise is anything but the common lot: "The odds are twenty to one when a poor man makes a throw in the world's play. . . . Twenty to one against poverty, always" (145).

As the blackening of Sip suggests, when a poor woman rolls the dice, the odds are even worse. Urged by Perley to find a new and less onerous form of employment, Sip resists, claiming that it is "too late" for her to leave the mills. "It's in the blood," she insists, pointing to the factory folk of England: "From father to child, from children to children's children,—

the middle class eludes us because it identifies not a bounded position between a plebeian working class and an aristocratic upper class but rather a pervasive cultural norm. That norm emerged as those domestic ideals taken to be resident in the private home and embodied in genteel white women translated themselves into a dominant set of values and styles of living. Cutting across the bipartite division that purportedly rent American society, the middle class manifested itself in new styles and manners, in the rituals of daily life, in the parlor and in the novel.

It is precisely in the parlor scene—in the account of an evening entertainment at Perley's "lofty, luxurious" Five Falls house—that we become most conscious of the middle-class sensibility that shapes *The Silent Partner*. The purpose of the evening is to bring labor and capital face-to-face. Thirty millworkers, all "in decent clothes," are invited to join a cluster of Perley's well-heeled Boston friends for an evening of music, ice cream, and dramatic reading. The Scottish novelist Margaret Oliphant, reviewing *The Silent Partner* in 1871 for *Blackwood's Magazine*, commented acidly on Perley's "little tea parties": "A most truly American and young-lady-like way of making the spinners happy," she observed.[41] The happiness of the spinners is not, however, the point of the scene, nor even its most American attribute. Rather, Perley's soiree is intended as a lesson in democratic equality. Take the spinners out of the mills, dress them in the "best suits" all Americans—regardless of station—manage to have, and put them in a parlor, and they do not, the narrator claims, "leave a very different impression" from that left by any thirty people who might gather at a Boston musicale.

This claim is as remarkable in the context of Phelps's novel as it is commonplace in the culture of midcentury. It would seem not only to undo the work of representation, directed as it is toward elaborating class difference, but to suggest that class conflict can be averted by occasional interclass sociability. "Going into Society," the chapter's title, seems at first glance to refer to the workers' attendance at the soiree, but this assumption is misguided. The title refers, instead, to leaving the precincts of wealth and privilege and going out into the world: going into society, not "Society," as Perley makes clear. But this last meaning is undermined by the account of the soiree. While the condition of labor remains a nominal subject of discussion—Sip tells the assembled guests about the summer heat in the weaving room and ridicules a newspaper account of life in the Lorenzo mills; Bijah Mudge rants about the ten-hour day—the working-class characters are clearly admitted into the parlor on the condition that they mimic the dress and manners of their social betters. "Society" does not accommodate them; they conform to its requirements, thus enabling the successful encounter between rich and poor. Finding their better selves mirrored in the millworkers, the wealthy are recalled to virtue, their dominance intact. They need not confront the difference between themselves and the workers, much less the ugliness of the life of labor, but only a new and improved version of themselves, for the common humanity of capital and labor is demonstrated by labor's appreciation of the things of capital—most especially their appreciation of the "superior" art produced by a leisured class of which they are not a part. The norms of dress and behavior to which the workers at the soiree conform, like the art that is applauded there by millions and mills alike, belong to a class whose universality goes unquestioned in the novel.

Perley's soiree makes us acutely conscious of the middle-class narrator whose voice directs our responses in *The Silent Partner*. The bitterly ironic tone of the descriptions of the self-indulgent rich and the earnest sympathy expressed for the embattled poor serve to locate the narrator outside the very dualities of class that define Perley and Sip. Claiming the high moral ground of the disinterested observer, the narrator advances a set of ideals typically inscribed in the middle-class household—from simplicity of dress to a well-ordered domesticity to sincere Christian feeling and benevolent activity on behalf of the poor.

But if the voice and values of the narrator immediately identify her as middle class, they no less immediately identify her as female. And it is by means of that female narrator's governing consciousness that change becomes possible in *The Silent Partner*. The gulf between labor and capital can be bridged after all, it seems, by universalizing middle-classness and naturalizing gender. Abandoning the divisive binaries that constitute social identity, Phelps finds the ground for a common identity in the femaleness—and by extension, the shared middle-class ethos—of her characters. This shift moves the problem of class out of history and into nature; the answer to the arbitrary impositions of class lies in the nature of "woman," a nature that seeks expression even in the face of the distortions of class. Likewise, this shift moves the novel out of the historical frame provided by the debate over capital and labor and into a different frame, this one shaped by the history of the elusive, pervasive, and feminized middle class.

Even as the portraits of Perley and Sip open the prospect of class conflict, the plot of *The Silent Partner*, governed as it is by the middle-class narrator, moves irresistibly toward harmonizing the differences that separate them by rendering these differences inessential—or anyway inconsequential by comparison to their identity in nature. On opposite sides in the war between labor and capital, Sip and Perley are nonetheless offered, provisionally at least, as natural allies; their friendship figures a harmony of interests more natural by virtue of its origin in gender and more transcendent in its moral claims than any founded on economic interest. Both are orphans, both refuse marriage, both struggle with the bequests of their fathers, however different. They are, moreover, allied in their efforts to

improve the condition of labor, in their devotion to Sip's deformed sister
Catty,[42] in their exclusion from power, in their disinterested Christianity.
The gulf that separates Perley and Sip is to be bridged, then, by their
shared womanhood—which, in this case, turns out to be an alternative
rendering of class, for it is as versions of the middle-class white woman
that Perley and Sip are proposed as sisters. If the impossibility of economic
mobility precludes a harmony of interests in the workplace, the stability
of gender across class lines can nonetheless assure the more perfect harmony of "home," in the parlor and the heart alike.

In a clear effort to find in Perley and Sip's equality as women the answer
to class inequality, Phelps, violating the usual domestic scheme and abandoning marriage as the figure of harmony, reconfigures the opposition
between capital and labor as an opposition between men and women.
The oppression of labor is accomplished by men like Maverick Hayle, the
junior partner, who blink at the violation of child labor laws, ignore the
condition of the tenements for which their employees pay them rent, claim
that they "cannot afford . . . experiments in philanthropy" (SP, 135), and
believe that "Master and man meet on business grounds, and business
grounds alone" (136). Motivated solely by profit, men control a world
that silences Perley and Sip alike. Both the oppression of labor and the
oppression of women are the doing of men. Women, on the contrary,
insofar as they allow themselves (or are permitted) to feel, feel right, as
Harriet Beecher Stowe predicted they would. Moreover, the disinterested
demands of conscience urged by feeling propel them out of the home and
into the world to right the wrongs they find there. Unable by virtue of
their sex to fully inhabit the positions to which they are relegated by the
language of capital and labor, Perley and Sip are relocated in a position
marked by the commonality of gender.

What I mean to suggest is that, faced with the recalcitrance of class,
Phelps turns to a vision of women empowered by a disinterested morality
to bring harmony to a world rent apart by the selfishness of men. Her
feminist critique of women's places in (or outside of) the scheme of production leads to the assertion of gender solidarity as the basis for a new
social order. Thus, awakened to the condition of labor, Perley suffers an
internal revolution that supplants the need for a social one. "I cannot tell
you how the world has altered to me," she explains to her puzzled but,
as always, admiring fiancé, "nor how I have altered to myself . . . these
people seem to have been thrust upon my hands—as empty, idle, foolish
hands, God knows, as ever he filled with an unsought gift" (SP, 139).
Assuming her God-given responsibility for the millworkers, Perley re-
nounces her life of leisure. Giving up her house in town, her place on "the
best pew list in Five Falls," and her "duty to Society," she dedicates herself
to building model tenements, establishing libraries for the edification of

the working class, nursing the sick, and converting the wicked. She becomes, as she puts it, "not a reformer" but a "feeler"; she becomes, that is, a true woman.

This shift in the frame governing the novel is reflected in its structure. While the first half of the novel is taken up with vignettes exposing the injustices of wage slavery—Bub Mell's death in the machinery, the blacklisting of Bijah Mudge, the wickedness of Dib Docket, the temptation of Nynee Mell—the second half is replete with images of reconciliation and redemption. In an episode that the narrator, in one of her few intrusions into her story, insists she was "urged . . . to find a place for . . . although it is fragmentary and incomplete" (SP, 243), the workers at the Hayle and Kelso mill threaten to strike after their wages are reduced. "Uneasy like the rest" of the owners, Perley urges that the partners send Stephen Garrick, newly risen from the ranks of labor to the position of partner, to the mill yard to "tell them *why* we must reduce their wages" (248). This expedient proves unsuccessful, and at the workers' demand, Perley herself goes out to speak to them. With her appearance, we are told, comes "a sudden tide of respectability": oaths, brickbats, and rum disappear, and silence falls on the crowd standing in the rain and mud. Reiterating Garrick's claims about the necessity of lowering wages, Perley arrests the strike before it has properly begun. "It's not that they so much disbelieved Mr. Garrick," we learn later from Sip, "but when *she* said she couldn't afford to pay 'em, they believed *that*" (252).

Standing "so quiet," "so white and still," with "a shining to her," Perley by her mere presence shames the workers into renouncing their decision to strike. The response of Reuben Mell, in which an echo of Hawthorne's "laboring men" can be heard, is typical: "It's very perplexing to me. It doesn't mean a dollar's worth less of horses and carriages, and grand parties to the Company, such a trouble as this don't seem to. And it means *we* go without our breakfast so's the children sha'n't be hungry. . . . That's what reduction o' wages means to *us*. I don't understand the matter myself, but . . . I'll take the young leddy's word for it, this time" (SP, 253). Just as the reasons for the "fragmentary" nature of the account go unexplained, so neither Perley nor the narrator offers an answer to Reuben Mell's dilemma. Just as remarkable, given the novel's beginning, no challenge is offered to Perley's anti-labor position. Instead, the "flood-tide" that threatens Hayle and Kelso simply ebbs away, leaving behind its flotsam and jetsam, a "few small boys" and a drunk.

Marked off by the narrator's initial disclaimers and offered primarily as "indicative" of Perley's character, this incident is not, in the last analysis, about the strike at all, but rather about the spiritual power to restore harmony invested in true womanhood. Paradoxically, at the one moment in the novel when Perley speaks publicly—the only moment in which the silent partner is invested with a voice—we are told almost nothing of what she says. Moreover, what we are told we cannot but regard as deeply compromised. For although Sip admires Perley's efforts, their alliance is betrayed by Perley's efforts to put down the strike despite the apparent legitimacy of labor's position. Class interest, it would seem, outweighs gender solidarity in the end. But, then, what Perley says to the strikers is not the point of the chapter in which her words appear. The point, instead, lies in the power of her altogether female presence, as the title of the chapter suggests: "Maple Leaves" refers not to the strike at all but to the romantic autumnal walk that follows it, in the course of which Perley refuses to become Stephen Garrick's "silent partner."

The problem of *The Silent Partner* is set by the rigid distinction of capital and labor, but the solution we are offered lies in the ethos of a middle class whose boundaries are permeable, whose ideals are universal, whose representatives are female, and whose existence goes unacknowledged. Ultimately, the effort to displace class antagonism with gender solidarity and thus generate a solution to the problem of class fails. Not only is maternity, the conventional source of a female social ethos, complicated by the determined singleness of Phelps's characters,[43] but the changed and heightened social consciousness that enables the identification of women across class lines emerges as itself a prerogative of class.

Perley's character is defined by change—change of heart, of circumstances, of residence, of taste, of behavior—but Sip's fate remains sealed. In fact, while Perley's change of heart is enabled by her identification with Sip, who provides both motive and means for her benevolent activity, that same change of heart reinscribes the distance between the lady and the factory girl. For it is not, finally, her femaleness but her class status that frees Perley to reinvent herself—and to redirect the resources she commands by virtue of that status. Representing Perley's powerlessness as the result of her passive but voluntary acquiescence to the false demands made upon women by social position, Phelps can at least in part remedy Perley's largely spiritual predicament. Perley can, in other words, be turned from fashionable to womanly just as her money can be turned from the purchase of sandalwood scent for her carriage to the purchase of beefsteak for undernourished workers.

But not so Sip. She is doomed to remain a factory worker by the very "syntax" that defines her. Despite the narrator's efforts to indicate that Sip, too, is a woman—and a woman like Perley—by invoking her self-sacrificing love for her sister, her sensitive appreciation of the arts, her sexual continence, and her Christian faith, Sip cannot be saved from the mills. As long as her "manful" struggle remains an economic necessity and remains, moreover, an essential feature of the novel's "truth," her nature as woman must remain potential only. Just as Maverick's language of masters and men writes the working-class woman out of existence, so the language of middle-class feminism cannot render the particularity of Sip's life as a mill girl.

Thus at the novel's close, when Sip is given her turn to speak publicly, we are recalled to the inevitability of her position, to her exclusion from the middle-class luxury that supports Perley's philanthropy and allows her to grow into "womanhood." Inspired by the mute Catty's "words"— words that turn out to be none other than God's—Sip takes up street preaching and, like Perley in the strike scene, she too discourages social action, urging instead reliance on Christ. But the importance of the scene lies less in Sip's conventional resort to a feminine faith of the heart in the face of economic injustice than in the reprise of the original representational scheme of the novel.

Whereas Perley has become "healthy" and "happy," her "womanly, wonderful face . . . beg[ging] for nothing" but "opulent and warm" with "life brimming over at it" (SP, 302), Sip remains, for all her faith, poor and dark. "A little rough, brown girl" with "nothing saintly" about her (294), even in the throes of inspiration, Sip's face is a "lighted, dark" one (300). Perley attends Sip's sermon, held "in a little court, a miserable place, breaking out like wart from one of the foulest alleys in Five Falls" (293), with Fly, the new Mrs. Maverick Hayle and the same companion who accompanies her to the opera in the opening scene of the novel. Sip is wholly unconscious of Perley's presence; in fact, the only person of whom we know her to be aware is Nynee Mell, now the wife of her onetime suitor. A weaver to the end, Sip addresses the mill operatives in a sermon built around the conceit of weaving. The "tangle" of class, in which "the great and the small . . . are all snarled," she declaims, requires Christ for its "unwinding"; "Kings and congresses . . . [g]overnments and churches" may "finger us over," but "we'll only snarl the more" (299). In the context of the narrator's fearful invocation of the "black reef" and the striking "hand," the double entendre is conspicuous, if not conscious. Like the "tangle" of class, without Christ the voice of labor remains a "snarl."

Class divisions, it would seem, are irremediable except perhaps by supernatural intervention, and class affiliation is as inescapable as class harmony is improbable. No words pass between Sip and Perley in this final scene. Their partnership is at an end: "I undertook to help her at the first," Perley explains to Fly, "but I was only *among* them at best; Sip is *of* them . . . so I left her to her work, and I keep to my own" (SP, 293). Leaving "the little preacher still speaking God's words" in the foul alley between shifts at the mill, the redeemed Perley, whose spiritual renovation turns out to be the raison d'être of the novel, returns to her new life outside of class. Separated from the wage slave Sip by the "fixed gulf of an irreparable lot," Perley is, at the end, likewise conscious of the "impassable gulf" that yawns between herself and "a pretty, good-natured little lady" like the wealthy and fashionable Fly. Just as she can be, at most, among the workers but not of them, so too she is now only among the rich. No longer the embodiment of idle capital and now excluded too from the life of labor, Perley exploits the resources of the first in the interest of the last. She marks the place of an ideal middle class.

Chapter IV

BEGINNING AGAIN

Love, Money, and a Circle of "Friends"

Twenty-two years after New York's chief of police issued his hyperbolic report on the city's "infestation" of street urchins, Charles Loring Brace tried to alert his genteel fellow citizens to the threat posed by *The Dangerous Classes of New York*. "It has been common," he explained, "since the recent terrible Communistic outbreak in Paris, to assume that France alone is exposed to such horrors; but, in the judgment of one who has been familiar with our 'dangerous classes' for twenty years, there are just the same explosive social elements beneath the surface of New York."[1] Brace is blunt about the nature of these explosive elements. The "thousands and thousands in New York who have no assignable home" comprise a great mass of "destitute, miserable, and criminal persons." Beholding "the gilded rewards of toil . . . but . . . never permitted to touch them," the homeless and impoverished recognize that "for ages the rich have had all the good things of life, while to them have been left the evil things," and conclude, according to Brace, that "Capital . . . is the tyrant" (29).

New Yorkers who imagine their city immune to the "horrors" of the Paris Commune, Brace insists, not only fail to appreciate the volatility of the destitute masses but, more alarmingly, repress their own recent history. The "desperate multitude"—composed not only of men but, to Brace's great distress, of "*women*"—who rioted in 1863[2] and again in the early 1870s may have taken "unoffending negroes" or Protestant "Orangemen" as their proximate targets, but it was "evident to all careful observers," he claims, that, unchecked, their "attack would have been directed at the apparent wealth of the city—the banks, jewelry shops, and rich private homes" (30). In 1872, New York, with its all-too-obvious extremes of poverty and wealth, its increasing dependence on waged work, and its escalating labor agitation, appeared to Brace, as to others, perilously close to class warfare.

But of all the "dangerous classes" that threatened urban America, the most dangerous of all remained Matsell's "distinctively homeless" children, whose numbers Brace estimates at twenty to thirty thousand in New York alone. Luckily, the condition of these "children of poverty and vice" is not, he claims, as it is for their European counterparts, "fixed and inherited" (26), but susceptible to remedy. Yet if their criminal tendencies are "not so deeply stamped in the blood," these children nonetheless partake of another, a national, inheritance. In "every fibre," Brace maintains, they express the "intensity of the American temperament": "their crimes have the unrestrained and sanguinary character of a race accustomed to overcome all obstacles" (27).

The most dangerous, then, but also paradoxically the most salvageable members of the dangerous classes, these "young ruffians" of the streets combine the ignorance and brutality of those forced to " 'flit' from attic . . . to cellar," to sleep in boxes on the street or "swarm" in tenement houses, with a characteristically "American" faith in their own success. According to Brace, it is precisely because they do not, unlike Sip, believe themselves doomed by their "blood" to unending poverty that the American poor are driven to "murder, where European *proletaires . . .* fight with fists," and are prepared to "begin . . . the sacking of a city, where English rioters would merely batter policemen, or smash lamps" (27). In a stroke of brilliance, Brace uses nationality to bring class orthodoxy and class heresy into an altogether new relationship: the promise of mobility, widely touted as the foundation of class harmony, is reconfigured instead as the catalyst of class conflict.

Unless, of course, that promise is made tangible, and the *"enfants perdus"* saved from "hardship, penury, and unceasing drudgery" (Brace 31). Charity, Brace acknowledges, originates "in CHRIST," but its urgent purpose is nonetheless social, not spiritual. That purpose is to provide the opportunity for mobility to the "outcast street-children" of the underclass, children who, however poor, are Americans and therefore brook no obstacles in their pursuit of success. Philanthropic intervention must be undertaken, he urges, if those with a vested interest in the social order hope to avert "an explosion . . . which might leave this city in ashes and blood" (29). The gulf between poverty and wealth, between the mills and the millions, must be closed. What is more, it can be closed, if reformers will only turn their attention from adults to children—from the already lost to the yet to be saved, from the already classed, as it were, to those whose class position is, Brace insists, not yet fixed.

The reprise of the antebellum domestic novel and its vision of social harmony in the postwar juvenile fiction of Horatio Alger Jr. and in the work of Louisa May Alcott is less surprising than it might otherwise be when set alongside Brace's account of the activities of his Children's Aid Society. In part an organizational history written to encourage philanthropists everywhere to "inaugurate comprehensive and organized movements for the improvement of their 'Dangerous Classes,' " *The Dangerous Classes of New York* is equally, and more importantly for my purposes, a collection of "little stories of the lot of the poor in cities" (Brace, iii). Drawn from Brace's journal and from his wide correspondence, these stories simultaneously give evidence of the social evils that attend the children of the urban poor and serve a mediatory function. Like the charitable work they describe, they are meant to avert class violence not only by "bring-[ing] the two ends of society nearer together in human sympathy" (iii) but by insisting that it is the "poor" and not an unjustly oppressed class of workers that is at issue. Although they are not invariably optimistic in tone, these stories, for the most part, share a common plot in which the dire conditions of the urchin's life are, first, laid out and then assuaged by charitable intervention. Typical is Brace's outraged account of one "thin, sad," vermin-ridden "street arab."[3] "Within two blocks of our richest houses," an appalled Brace exclaims, "a desolate boy grows up, not merely out of Christianity and out of education, but out of a common human shelter, and of means of livelihood" (321). Taken in hand by a charity worker, he is, "after a thorough washing and cleansing," dispatched to Illinois, where, as is often the case in these tales, he is adopted by an "old gentleman of property, who, being childless . . . will make him an heir to a property" (321).

The orphan does not, it is worth noting, inherit the whole of the old gentleman's property but only a sufficiency, enough for the boy to make a start in his own rise to prosperity. Brace's narratives are not, after all, extravagant fictions in which poor boys ascend to great wealth solely by means of their altogether excellent character and the aid of gentlemen, but rather "true" stories meant to authenticate the dangers that inhere in the urban conditions he describes and to demonstrate the individual and collective benefits of charity. But if Brace's "little stories" are factual, they nonetheless bear a close resemblance to Horatio Alger's fictions. Given Alger's association with the Children's Aid Society as well as with the other preeminent charity for boys in New York, the Newsboys' Lodging House, this similarity is not surprising. Like Brace, Alger took the homeless boys of the streets as his special subject and their respectable brothers as his audience. Peopled with bootblacks, newsboys, match boys, the fiddlers and organ-grinders victimized by the padrone system[4]—the best of them "attractive," "frank . . . manly and self-reliant"[5] despite their circumstances—as well as with "interested" gentlemen of property, confidence men, and thieves, his books paint an urban world riven by class and redeemed by the affection of men.

As early as the 1850s, arbiters of genteel taste like *Graham's Magazine* and *Godey's Lady's Book* had already begun to bemoan the proliferation of metropolitan novels about "rag-pickers, lamp-lighters, foundlings, beggars, rogues," seeing an incitement to social unrest in their tendency not only to mitigate the "mendacity and vice" of the poor but to cast their unfortunate protagonists as victims of injustice.[6] Such novels could, of course, be redeemed by a turn from shoes to kittens of the kind we have seen in *The Lamplighter*, a turn from the heretical possibility of class antagonism to the harmony of the home over which the girl protagonist presides. That scheme, as I have already suggested, frames class harmony as the outcome of an ideal and putatively classless gender conformity and, further, binds the mobility that obviates class conflict tightly to heterosexual marriage.

But if in antebellum novels like *The Lamplighter* or *The House of the Seven Gables* the culminating marriage of the self-possessed young woman to the promising young man could unproblematically adumbrate a larger class harmony, by the 1860s the representations of feminist reformers and of labor activists alike "proletarianized"[7] the poor, greatly complicating the fictional portrayal of engagement across class lines. Invoking a universal sisterhood that nonetheless demanded conformity to bourgeois standards of virtue, "the language of feminism," Christine Stansell has argued, "subsumed working-class women's experience into the category of victimization."[8] Feminism, that is to say, simultaneously acknowledged and repudiated class difference; sisterhood extended not to the limits of gender but to those of respectability. Benighted victims of industry, working-class women were projected not as independent agents but, at best, as simulacra of an imitable middle class and, at worst, as "vicious" and unredeemable. But if the language of mid-nineteenth-century feminist reform could not credit genuinely divergent class cultures, it equally could not credit a perfect community of interests between women and men. The dangers of class might be countered by the domestication of the Bowery g'hal or her orphan sister, but as *The Silent Partner* suggests, for middle-class, white feminists absorbed in struggles over marriage, property rights, citizenship, and work, heterosexual domesticity could no longer figure a wider social harmony.

The gender ideology that informed the arguments for the family wage launched by midcentury labor activists similarly disrupted standing novelistic strategies. Remanding working women to the home and subsuming "the particularities of their lives into the unified interests of the working-class family" (Stansell, 220), the language of class solidarity imagined away conflict between men and women. Yet the community of interests represented by marriage and the family in the discourse of class struggle attested not to a larger harmony of interests across class lines but instead to the endogamous class loyalty essential to that struggle.

By the eve of the Civil War, gender identity had become "a contested issue in conflicts of class" (Stansell, 219). The obverse was likewise true, as class identity came to figure in increasingly problematic ways in the struggle over women's rights. For middle-class industrial novelists like Rebecca Harding Davis and Elizabeth Stuart Phelps who sought literary and political representation for their working-class subjects, the impossibility of "untangling" class was, if anything, confirmed by the failure of gender solidarity to rise above the exigencies of class. Davis's lovelorn Deb feels her heartbreak as deeply as any lady, Davis assures us, but however much sympathy her unrequited love for Hugh Wolfe may garner from genteel readers, this democratic extension of feminine feeling to include the working-class woman does not improve Deb's life chances.[9] Likewise, Phelps's portrayal of Perley's attempt to close the gulf between capital and labor through cross-class, same-sex friendship flounders not only because Sip and Perley cannot be brought to inhabit equally the prosperous world that enables "womanly" virtue but because, having proposed gender difference as an analogue to class antagonism, the novel can find no satisfactory way to address either. Believing both herself and the children she refuses to bear to be doomed to the mills, Sip may be a sister but she is no less a weaver for that.

The feminist analogy between class and gender oppressions of the kind employed by Phelps in *The Silent Partner* not only precludes heterosexual union as an image of class harmony but has other, more complicated literary effects as well. Insofar as the irrevocability of gender difference—and, in the case of Sip, racialized difference—informs the consideration of the industrial worker, this analogy effectively disallows economic mobility as the basis for a commonality of interests, thus banishing the prospect of class harmony. Raised from the tenement stoop to the parlor, and raised too from child to woman, Gerty Flint can, by coming into spiritual possession of herself, come as well to possess the stuff of bourgeois respectability: a home, a husband, and an income. No such rise is possible in *The Silent Partner*. Instead, Phelps's female couple—representatives, respectively, of middle-class womanhood and working-class fortitude—come into possession of a new consciousness of the operation of gender and class, a consciousness that simultaneously alerts them to the possibility of female solidarity and heightens their awareness of the unalterable difference between workers and women.

My point is that the figure of the "proletarianized" worker cannot support a narrative of ascent: for the working-class girl, gender is a liability, not, as it is for the poor but unclassed Gerty, an asset. In fact, literary proletarianization, relying as it does on the construction of character around what are imputed as fixed class attributes and the construction of plot around the apparently irremediable conditions of industry, blocks the forward motion of narrative altogether. Even when they do not die, like Hugh Wolfe or Phelps's Bub Mell, characters identified with the industrial working class remain immured in the dank cellars and foul alleys to which they are driven by the "millions" who exploit their labor.

To reclaim the domestic novel, as Alger attempted to do, is to reclaim the narrative of ascent and, with it, emphatically to reassert the innocence of the "dangerous classes" of class itself. Beginning again with the home-less orphan, the poor boy whose location in the streets of an all-male city purged of all evidence of a working class obviates his location in class, Alger banishes the effects of the industrial wage system and the impera-tives of heterosexuality alike and turns instead to a new kind of home as the origin and reward of endeavor in a free market.

Alger may have been the greatest promoter of the poor but promising bootblack, but he invented neither this figure nor the all-male, interclass universe he inhabits. A decade before he appeared in *Ragged Dick* (1867), the first and the most successful of Alger's famous boy's books,[10] the image of the "frank, straightforward," and "decidedly good-looking" (40) bootblack had already graced the pages of such periodicals as *Frank Leslie's Illustrated Newspaper* and *Harper's Weekly*. Impudent, cocksure, and almost always barefoot, these bootblacks—all of them white, despite the traditional predominance of African Americans in the bootblacking trade[11]—are pictured quipping with their customers, lounging on street corners, and energetically accosting fashionable gentlemen. They are poorly dressed, though not usually in rags, and their promise is suggested by the energy with which they are represented as plying their trade as well as by their apparent self-reliance. In fact, as representations—or represen-tatives—of the most dangerous of the dangerous classes, these popular images of street urchins fail abysmally. They bear no signs of corruption, nor do they seem, in the manner of the illustrations in *The Dangerous Classes* or the later photographs of Jacob Riis and Lewis Hine, demoral-ized or deformed by their destitution. On the contrary, like Ragged Dick himself, the plucky American bootblack, presented so matter-of-factly as a feature of the urban scene in the illustrated press of the 1850s, is a figure disturbing to middle-class sensibilities only insofar as self-sufficiency in children signifies homelessness and as bare feet signify poverty.

In animating the image of the bootblack, Alger plays out scenes similar to those pictured in the popular periodicals. Like the cartoon bootblacks, Ragged Dick disdains the vanity of the "heavy swell," is amused by the gullible country bumpkin, observes the doings of the street with insouci-ance, and competes heartily for "shines." But Dick's humorous and good-humored engagement with the urban scene does not disguise the fact that the problem he presents is, at base, the same problem that is posed by Cummins's Gerty. Barefoot, dirty, and ignorant, Dick is, despite his sharp wit and his street wisdom, yet another orphan in need of a home. And

Alger, like Cummins, must persuade his readers—middle-class boys, in this case, rather than their mothers or sisters—of his orphan's "good points," of his potential for inclusion in their respectable midst. Substituting boyish pluck for girlish pathos and Dick's sassy nonchalance for Gerty's belligerence, Alger sets about recovering the domestic novel for the purposes of boys and, with it, a world in which homeless boys can rise. Neither a girl whose femininity is sufficient to summon a home nor an American *proletaire* bent on taking his home by storm, Alger's orphan must earn his home in a market world in which enterprising boys and interested gentlemen conspire to bring about his success.

The regendering of the orphan's quest for a home, in other words, makes all the difference. Despite Alger's insistent use of the blurry categories of wealth and poverty and not those of class, his boy, unlike the orphan girl of the 1850s, must move through class, not out of it. Home is for him an economic achievement, not a spiritual one, the product of sound investment, not self-possession, and the reward of homosocial collaboration, not heterosexual marriage. In fact, insofar as it comes to figure the perfect harmony of interests underwritten by mobility, domesticity in *Ragged Dick* both depends on and enables the apparently universal commitment of boys (and men) to their economic betterment and thus to one another. Beginning, like *The Lamplighter*, with a shoeless urchin, abandoned in infancy to the care of an impoverished landlady by the death of his mother and left, like Gerty, at the age of seven to fend for himself, *Ragged Dick* similarly traces the orphan's rise to respectability through strenuous effort and the charitable interventions of the rich. But whereas in *The Lamplighter* the displacement of class by gender—the substitution of a masculinizing poverty with what might, anachronistically, be called a gentrifying femininity—anticipates and ultimately accomplishes the poor girl's rise into the middle class, class and gender operate in tandem in the capitalist world of *Ragged Dick*.

Thus it is not insignificant that Gerty is set apart from the "rude herd" of local urchins, while Ragged Dick stands at the center of a congeries of bootblacks. More honest than some, more generous than others, livelier and more quick-witted than most, he is surrounded by other boys from the moment we meet him being rousted out of his "Box Hotel" on Spruce Street. Alger's city streets provide the setting for an expansive homosocial fellowship, a community of boys encompassing a range of ethnic types, moral qualities, and individual temperaments. From the identifiably Irish and wholly unambitious Johnny Nolan—an unwilling object of charitable intervention[12]—and the belligerent gang leader Micky McGuire, whose ethnicity is signaled by the narrator's sly allusion to Tammany Hall, to the all-American Henry Fosdick, the timid but well-educated orphan of a prosperous printer, and the native-born Tom Wilkins, the sole support of an ailing mother, these boys, for all their differences, are driven by poverty to share the streets. But the very heterogeneity of the fellowship of bootblacks—their ultimate inequality of opportunity—stands as one kind of evidence that, unlike Davis's "masses" of indistinguishable mill-workers, they do not constitute a class—and certainly not a doomed and brutalized working class. On the contrary, theirs is, the narrator makes clear, an affiliation based on shared boyhood.

In fact, lest we imagine Dick to belong to an oppressed proletariat, his independence as a street trader is established early in the novel. Self-employed, as it were, Dick's time is his own and his devotion to his "business" governed only by his need for food and his desire for entertainment. A free agent successfully engaged in competitive enterprise, Dick is, at one extreme, the antithesis of the desperate, downtrodden Hugh Wolfe and, at the other, the opposite in his whiteness of Webb's Charlie Ellis, who suffers no lack of enterprise but whose promise is thwarted by his color. Unlike these others, Dick is exactly a boy who may "make himself anything he chooses."[13] The youthful embodiment of an ideal white republican manhood—an ideal increasingly illusory by the time of his creation—Dick is the promising boy revivified. "Manly" and "self-reliant" beyond his years, endowed with a natural sense of justice and fair play, and "attractive" to boot, Dick lacks only an image of his future success. Convinced that he will "grow up to be a vagabone . . . and come to the gallows" (75), he, not unreasonably, regards any alternative future as a joke. The "manshun on Fifth Avenoo" to which Dick facetiously—and repeatedly—alludes, the grandiose flights of fancy about buying out retail magnate A. T. Stewart or sharing the financial anxieties of John Jacob Astor that punctuate his account of his life on the streets—these map an urban landscape in which the respectable middle class to which the reader believes Dick might reasonably aspire is eclipsed by stunning extremes of wealth and poverty.

But it is not Dick's character alone that saves him from the ranks of the proletariat, for despite the increasingly visible effects of industrialization in the New York of the 1860s, the working class—and particularly working-class men—is conspicuously absent from Alger's city. Dick's tour of Manhattan, occupying fully a quarter of the novel and carrying the reader from the cheap clothing stores of Chatham Street to the "palaces" of Fifth Avenue, includes not a single industrial workplace.[14] Noting features of architectural and human interest, Dick does not omit "low" places and people from his tour—Barnum's freak show and the Old Bowery Theater, notable for its working-class melodramas, a "hideous" old apple peddler, porters, hawkers, and newsboys, and a full complement of con artists all appear—but factories and workshops are nowhere to be seen and neither are the men and women who labor in them. Purged of all signs of a laboring class doomed to oppression—or worse still, slated for rebellion—the city itself, as Alger draws it, mirrors the as yet unrecognized promise of the boy who lives on its streets.

The absence of the proletarianized worker is crucial to the logic of Alger's narrative. In order to recover the possibility of Dick's ascent to respectability, Alger must render his poverty accidental, not structural, the consequence of his orphaning, not of his oppression at the hands of a capitalist class. In what might appear to be a tautology, the recuperation of the domestic as an answer to the rising threat of class conflict requires that the absence of home rather than the presence of industry explain Dick's impoverished condition. Excising all signs of an industrial wage system from the very urban settings in which its impact was becoming increasingly visible, Alger reconstitutes a mercantile New York in which the benevolent paternalism of prosperous gentlemen and the deference of poor boys are conjoined in the endless reproduction of the narrative of mobility.

Alger's New York, in which waged work is in no way implicated in the production of poverty and in which boys band together in affection, not desperation, to form friendships, not trade unions, provides the conditions necessary to the poor boy's rise to prosperity. But it is Dick's success as a street trader that ensures that rise. For all his rags, Dick hovers on the brink of respectability even when we first meet him. Already earning as much as the "young clerks" who employ him in "his professional capacity" (43)—the morally ambiguous but nonetheless quintessential representatives of an emerging white-collar workforce[15]—and capable of earning substantially more than they, Dick can command the cash necessary to respectability. What he lacks is, on the one hand, a motive to industry—the set of desires that would prompt "rational" economic behavior—and, on the other, the image of a future self on which to trade and on the basis of which others might be brought to invest in his future. Instead of inhabiting the utopian marketplace in which the promising boy "buys" and sells the prospect of his own success, at the novel's opening, Dick occupies a continuous present, a gritty underworld of street urchins and con men gambling on immediate, short-term gain in which "However much he managed to earn during the day, all was . . . spent before morning" (43). But if Dick must learn to invest in his future in order to rise to respectability, he must first be able to imagine himself as a good investment. In this, the homosocial community of "good fellows" serves him admirably. Its members drawn together by their youth and their gender, not by the injustices of class, this capacious fellowship provides the basis not only for a sympathetic interclass alliance between bootblacks but for cross-class alliances between bootblacks and the boys best equipped to provide the tutelage they most need.

Others have commented on the linguistic proximity of speculation to the " 'spectability" Dick comes to desire, and the relationship of these, in turn, to the spectatorial.[16] The confluence of these terms is essential to Dick's early and formative encounter with Frank Whitney, the son of a "gentleman." In fact, the logic of that encounter—in which the prospect of respectability is revealed to Dick and its fulfillment is assured by the affectionate interest of another boy—establishes the relationship between outward appearance, sound investment, and male homosociality requisite to Dick's success. Loitering outside the Astor House hotel in hopes of finding custom, Dick overhears the young Frank Whitney voicing his disappointment at the fact that his industrious father has no time to show him the "sights of New York." "Being an enterprising young man," Dick instantly recognizes "a chance for a speculation" (55) and proposes himself as a guide. Gambling on the Whitneys' willingness to gamble on him, Dick's "novel proposition" calls Mr. Whitney's attention to the spectacle of poverty he presents. A "ragged figure," Dick is "not exactly the sort of guide" the gentlemanly but, as we learn, self-made Mr. Whitney would have chosen for his son. Nonetheless, Dick's honest looks and "open face" (55) persuade Whitney to take a chance.

These signs of good character, while they encourage Mr. Whitney to speculate on Dick's fitness as a guide, are not, however, sufficient for his son, whose bourgeois concern for appearances makes him "a little shy" about being seen with a companion "so ragged and dirty" (55). Frank's discomfort prompts his father to a further, more material investment in Dick. Invited into the Astor House by the generous Mr. Whitney, Dick is kindly instructed to wash his face, comb his hair, and don the "neat grey suit," shirt, stockings, and shoes Frank provides him. His Cinderella-like transformation[17] complete, Dick looks at himself in the mirror and is appropriately incredulous: "that isn't me, is it?" he exclaims; "Don't you know yourself?" Frank responds (58). Dick does not, of course, "know" himself. The boy in the mirror—a boy who "might readily have been taken for a young gentleman" like Frank Whitney, were his hands not still "red and grimy" from bootblacking (58)—is, in equal proportions, a complete stranger to him and a stranger he might someday, when his hands are clean, become.

Condensed into this brief sequence are the essential elements of the transformation of Ragged Dick, bootblack, into Richard Hunter, promising counting-room clerk. Not that Dick's new clothes and his new companion immediately solve the problem of his homelessness—he returns, of necessity, to the streets and to bootblacking at the end of his day with Frank—but as surely as they do for Gerty Flint, these provide the wherewithal to attain a home: a new stock-in-trade, as it were. Instead of a bootblacking box, Dick suddenly has a new and promising self, the evidence of which lies not simply in the spectacle of a " 'spectable" boy he sees in the mirror but in the interest Frank and Mr. Whitney take in him, in the willingness of genteel types like the Whitneys to invest in him and thus invest him with a future. Whether his attention is garnered by luck or by pluck, the kindly "interest" of the respectable gentleman in the poor but handsome boy, which in *Ragged Dick* invariably expresses itself in monetary form, establishes the perfect congruence of the affectional and the economic.

Supplanting conflict between classes—the hostility of millions and mills—with friendship between individual men, Alger's circular system ensures that profit and affection alike come to the honest and attractive urchin. No exchange is driven purely by the desire for profit, nor is any motivated exclusively by feeling; each entails both. Doubly transformative, then, male friendship simultaneously accomplishes the translation of poverty into promise and, likewise, secures for the homeless boy not merely a home but the ties of affection that make for a home of the better sort.

True to its beginnings, Dick's exchange with the Whitneys appears first as an economic transaction in which the alternative spectacles Dick presents—one ragged, the other " 'spectable"—frame two understandings of speculation: gambling, on the one hand, and investing, on the other. The difference between these two is carefully propounded for Dick's—and the reader's—edification. Gambling, one of Dick's besetting "faults," is roundly denounced. A losing proposition in every sense, its most predictable yields are debt and bad company. Investment, by contrast, describes the economic activity of those solidly respectable businessmen who take an "interest," both speculative and spectatorial, in poor boys. Demanding self-discipline above all else—the accumulation of capital, education, planning, and forethought—investment summons the rewarding virtues of the middle class as a counterweight to the "self-indulgence" to which boys such as Dick are prone. Like Cummins's Gerty, for whom self-control is an essential condition of respectability, Dick too must learn self-regulation, but because he is a boy, it is the economic self, not the emotional one, over which he must exert control. If he is to profit from the capital invested in him by the Whitneys—the new clothes as well as the five dollars Mr. Whitney pays him for his services—he must learn to husband his resources and attend to his appearance. In this he requires instruction.

Having glimpsed his future in the hotel mirror and, significantly, having left his bootblacking box behind, if only for a time, Dick is primed for instruction by the time he and Frank leave the Astor House on what is ostensibly a city boy's tour of New York undertaken for a country boy's amusement. As it turns out, the urban landscape through which Dick and Frank wander provides the necessary occasions for edification across class lines. And for both boys, the lesson to be learned is a lesson in the operation of class. Crudely put, the country-bred Frank, on his "first visit to the city" (54), learns that not everyone is like himself, and Dick, the city urchin, learns that anyone can be like Frank. The prototype of Alger's reader, Frank discovers not only the facts of poverty, as Dick's history reveals itself, but the necessity of caution as Dick exposes one confidence game after another. He is instructed in precisely the skill his city-bred father exercises when he scrutinizes Dick's "honest face," that is, the careful assessment of character, a skill demanded not only by the world of urban strangers but in particular by the intermingling of rich and poor in that world. In a series of highly theatrical encounters, Dick, employing stagy quips and ripostes, outwits the con artist, saves the country bumpkin, and turns the sour "lady, as she probably called herself" (92) who suspects him of theft into a figure of public ridicule for the benefit of his audience of one. But for every urban villain the unlettered but street-smart Dick unmasks with his cleverness, the sober and well-schooled Frank offers an earnest lesson in traditional republican virtues. Theirs is a meeting not only of city and country, poverty and prosperity, but of distinct class styles, as Bowery melodrama meets English folktale.

The novel's paradigmatic lesson in upward mobility takes the form of just such a tale. Midway through their tour of New York, Frank proffers the story of Dick Whittington—another ragged Dick—in an attempt to impress upon his skeptical companion the benefits of a "saving disposition." As Frank tells it, Whittington, a poor but thrifty boy, is offered a home in the servants' quarters of a sympathetic wealthy merchant. Observed by the merchant collecting "pins and needles that had been dropped" in hopes of eventually selling them, Whittington is given the opportunity to invest in a voyage. Possessing as merchandise nothing but a kitten he has received as a gift, he invests the kitten, which is, fortuitously, just what is most needed by the king of a rat-infested and hitherto unknown island. Purchased by the king for "a great quantity of gold," the kitten thus lays "the foundation of [Whittington's] fortune" (75), upon which foundation rests his later career as a "very rich" merchant and his eventual election to the position of Lord Mayor of London.

The difference between this kitten and the one that sets Gerty Flint's rise to respectability in motion is worth noting. In *The Lamplighter*, the kitten deflects our attention from questions of class to those of gender, from the fate of the impoverished orphan to the future of the orphan girl. No such displacement is required in order to set Dick Whittington—or Ragged Dick—on the path to prosperous respectability. Already possessing, despite their circumstances, the best traits of their sex, such boys need only capital and the helping hands of other men to turn those traits to their most profitable use. The kitten that elicits the tender feelings appropriate to women from the embittered Gerty, thereby proving her right to shoes and a home, is no object of sentimental attachment in the story of Dick Whittington. Instead, it is an asset to be traded for financial gain.

Yet just as Gerty greets the gift of a kitten with skepticism, so Ragged Dick quite reasonably doubts that "all the cats in New York" will make him mayor (75). Nonetheless, the story of the kitten sets him on the path to respectability as surely as the kitten itself does Gerty, if just as obliquely. His new friend's conviction that if he will only "try" he "may rise in some other way" has its intended effect (75). Taking to heart Frank's "hope" for him as well as his lessons in the importance of saving and investing, Dick "earnestly" commits himself to the pursuit of his promise.

While their friendship is framed in the language of commerce, it nonetheless quickly becomes clear that Ragged Dick and Frank Whitney are drawn to one another in other ways. Just as the linguistic slide from the speculative to the 'spectable and the spectatorial blurs the nature of transactions between men and boys, the "interest" they take in one another is likewise highly ambiguous, referring at the very least to concerns both economic and emotional—and hinting at the erotic.[18] Intimating that relationships among men might encompass far more than the commercial, this fusion of the emotional and the economic is essential to achieving respectability—to getting and making a home—in *Ragged Dick*, where the domestic partnership of boys serves to enable economic mobility and where mobility restores the prospect of social harmony that characterizes domestic fiction. The trajectory of such partnerships is marked out in the evolving friendship between Dick and young Whitney and fulfilled in the home Dick establishes with Henry Fosdick.

Having invested in Dick's new clothes and thus made him appear to be a boy like himself, Frank claims both the rights of a benefactor and the freedom of a friend to inquire not only into Dick's life history but into his feelings. "Very much interested" in Dick, he acts the part of a "patron." Eliciting from Dick an account of his struggles and his wasteful ways, he urges, in return, the Franklinesque virtues of hard work, education, economy, and clean living that will "make people have confidence" in Dick's future (89) and thus aid him in his rise to respectability. That "confidence" is not, of course, the misplaced trust solicited by the urban swindlers who appear at every turn in Alger's New York but rather the reliance which gentlemen like Mr. Whitney place in the appearance of promise.

But the interest Frank professes himself to feel in Dick equally takes the form of a demonstrative sympathy, a sympathy that makes Dick long to fulfill Frank's expectations of him. In response to Frank's puzzlement at the "good spirits" he apparently maintains in the face of cold and hunger, Dick confesses that he sometimes has "the blues." Pressed to elaborate, Dick admits that he feels the absence of "one friend," "somebody to care for [him]," to which Frank, "lightly laying his hand on Dick's shoulder," responds "I will care for you. . . . If you will let me" (99). The nature of this "caring" is not specified, but in the context of an interest that interweaves the economic and the emotional, Frank's gesture holds out the promise that all forms of caring might be encompassed in the relationship between boys.

Not surprisingly, given this compound interest, Dick closes the transaction with Frank and his father on a far different note than he opened it. Having approached the Whitneys "determined to avail himself" of a "chance for a speculation" (55), he is so "touched" by their interest that he initially refuses the returns on his speculation, making clear his preference for "care" over cold cash. But these are not, it quickly becomes clear, mutually exclusive. In fact, Dick's encounter with the Whitneys constitutes a demonstration of what might be the novel's most basic premise, namely, that among respectable men, friendship and financial advantage go hand in hand. When Mr. Whitney, remembering his own "friendless youth," offers Dick five dollars in payment for his services as a guide, Dick at first demurs, saying, "I haven't earned it" (111). But pressed to accept the money and urged to "repay it in the form of aid to some poor boy, who is struggling upward as you are now" once he is a "prosperous man" (111), Dick yields gratefully and, in yielding, takes on the obligation to fulfill the promise the Whitneys have reposed in him, to someday join the ranks of gentlemen on whose "interest" the fates of poor boys depend.

Nonetheless, on leaving "the presence of Frank," for whom "he had formed a strong attachment," Dick suffers a wave of "loneliness" (111). As he realizes, Frank's willingness to be his "one friend" is infeasible, however heartfelt. Both its cross-class character and its accidental nature guarantee that their friendship be short-lived. The impulse toward respectability, however, brings its own rewards, and Dick's desire for a "friend" to care for him does not go unanswered. Returned to the streets in the new clothes that mark his promise, he faces a dilemma: if he resumes his ragged "Washington" coat and "Napoleon" pants, he forfeits his newfound respectability; if he sleeps on the street in his new clothes, he will "spile" them—"and that wouldn't pay" (114). Bent on protecting the capital, both material and social, he has suddenly acquired, Dick discovers that he needs the home respectability dictates, a home his gentle-manly appearance and his five dollars in turn procure for him.

The dingy room Dick rents in a Mott Street boardinghouse is, of course, only the first step in his "advancement in the world" (114). The next is to transform his accommodation into a home in the better sense, a domestic setting in which bonds of affection guarantee and are guaranteed by a harmony of interests. Having acquired a place to live, that is to say, Dick still needs a "friend." And this need is answered almost immediately by the narrator, himself an interested and benevolent gentleman, through the introduction of Fosdick, a boy whose name alone suggests him as Dick's perfect match. It is not, however, Fosdick's name alone that makes him the ideal domestic partner for Dick. A respectable boy driven to boot-blacking by the death of his printer father, Fosdick is no less a version of Frank Whitney than of Dick, but a version of Frank whose reduced circumstances make him an appropriate—and available—object of Dick's interest. His "natural timidity" summons the "manly" Dick's "chivalrous feeling" (133). "Ill-fitted for the coarse companionship of the street boys" (133) and unsuited by temperament to competing for custom, Fosdick, even more acutely than Dick, needs someone to care for him, and Dick responds by proposing a "bargain."

The chivalrous feelings that prompt Dick to invite Fosdick to share his bed on the night of their meeting are, however, as entangled with specula-tive interest of the economic sort as his exchange with Frank Whitney, for the poor but well-educated Fosdick has, Dick discovers, the additional capital he most needs. His invitation to spend the night is only the prelude to a longer-term proposition. If Fosdick will instruct him in the "readin' and writin' " he needs in order to achieve respectability, Dick, in ex-change, will share his bed permanently and, what is more, pay the whole of the rent, thus providing Frank with the home address respectable em-ployers require of the boys whose services they engage. Their combined assets—Dick's money and Frank's education—and their common invest-ment in respectability will propel the two boys, drawn together by pov-erty, into the white-collar world.

The genteel upbringing, the knowledge of books and manners, that makes Fosdick an invaluable partner for a boy on the rise, insofar as these are signaled by effeminacy, also make him a suspiciously desirable partner for a boy longing for a "friend." "Smaller," "slighter," and far more timo-rous than Dick, the delicate and well-bred Fosdick, who "shrinks" from rude jokes and vulgar theatricals and earnestly sympathizes with his friend's difficulties, perfectly complements the masculine self-sufficiency of Dick.[19] For all the homoerotic possibilities implicit in the "marriage" of Dick and Fosdick, these are not, however, permitted to inflect, or infect,

Alger's story. On the contrary, the management of sexual possibilities inherent in the same-sex couple is as essential as the management of class
if their domestic arrangements are to secure their respectability. Any suggestion of an erotic attachment between Dick and Fosdick is scotched
almost immediately upon the striking of the "bargain." "Drawn" to Fosdick, as he was to Frank, by his "goodness," Dick, we are assured, takes
his next "important step toward securing . . . genuine respectability"
(141) when, on the verge of first getting into bed together, he joins Fosdick
in saying his prayers. The point here is not religiosity but the observance
of forms and, in particular, the forms of respectable childhood. We are
recalled to the fact that Dick and Fosdick are only boys—and boys who
want to be "good" at that. Dick cannot ridicule Fosdick's prayers, as the
narrator claims some boys would, without asserting their difference and
thus complicating his claim to a future respectability. The cozy vignettes
of the two studying together by lamplight or sharing their dreams for the
future that characterize the account of their life together through the third
volume of the *Ragged Dick* series—in which the "boys," now almost fully
grown and remuneratively employed, "adopt" a little boy to share their
"handsomely furnished" front room on St. Mark's Place[20]—are emphatically domestic and carefully insulated from any erotic charge.

The narcissistic interest of gentlemen in ragged boys—an interest that,
whatever else may be said of it, guarantees the replication of their altogether respectable selves—stands as the motive force behind the romanticized (and romantic) marketplace in which economic transactions provide
a cover for homoerotic engagement. In that marketplace, production, entailing as it does recognition of the existence of a working class, does not
figure. Instead, the endless reproduction of the mercantile middle class is
accomplished through the rescue from vagabondage of the honest but
enterprising lad by those more prosperous than himself, and the narcissism that yields both care and profit is reiterated again and again in the
male pairings on which Alger's novel depends. As complementary halves
of a single whole or as opposites, Dick and Frank, Dick and Fosdick, or,
alternatively, Dick and the bully, Micky McGuire,[21] or Dick and Jim
Travis, whose rooms in the Mott Street boardinghouse mirror one another,[22] reinstate the deep connection between homosociality and mobility, domesticity and success.

The community of white men and boys through which, in *Ragged Dick*,
affection and profit circulate freely provides a template for male relationships in an idealized urban market-world where the poor are unaccountably poor and the rich are self-made. That community provides everything Dick needs, from an education to a home to work of a respectable
sort. The scene of domestic affection is not cordoned off from the sites of

economic activity but, reconceived around the same-sex couple, stands not as the motive or the reward for success in the marketplace but rather as its source. By excluding from its field of vision both women and workers—by overriding the analogy between gender difference and class difference—*Ragged Dick* voids class conflict and imagines a new kind of home in which masculine affection and economic mobility—love, as it were, and money—work in tandem to ensure a perfect harmony.

.   .   .

In 1872, a year before the serialization of her nearly completed novel in Henry Ward Beecher's *The Christian Union*, Louisa May Alcott changed its title from *Success* to *Work*. The journal entry on the salvific effects of labor in which this change is recorded lends Alcott's announcement of the title change a certain self-mocking quality: "Got out the old manuscript of 'Success,' and called it 'Work.' " But the change itself is nonetheless telling.[23] *Success*, as one suspects Alcott knew, might be the title of a Horatio Alger novel, conjuring up as it does stories of promising young men on the rise. *Work*, by contrast, speaks to the recalcitrance of the material world, a world that, as Alcott was aware, did not serve women's ambitions nearly so well as men's. As a title, *Work* captures the difficulty of the novel's young white female protagonist's struggle to reconcile the requirements, both internal and external, of respectable femininity with the demands of employment in the period roughly from 1850 to 1870. Just as importantly, it conjures up the setting of that struggle, the world of waged work.

Written with great difficulty, by Alcott's own account, between 1861 and 1873, *Work: A Story of Experience*, as the novel was finally titled, begins by casting aside both the earnest sentimentality and the narrative trajectory of midcentury domestic fiction. Neither a lachrymose tale of hard-won self-control nor a painstaking account of the feminization of the rebellious orphan in anticipation of her middle-class marriage, it inaugurates instead a new plot for a new girl, a girl who "shan't cry but act." Rightly, then, literary critics have been inclined to regard *Work* as "a deliberate unsettling of convention and expectation," affirming what Alcott's earlier and enormously popular *Little Women* "ultimately has to deny . . . the possibility of growth in female community."[24] While the latter moves inexorably away from the possibilities of same-sex community and toward marriage and maternity, replacing the sorority of March girls with a gathering of spouses, parents, and children, *Work* as decidedly reverses that progress. Opening with an explicit repudiation of marriage, dependence, and domesticity, it closes with the image of a "loving league of sisters, old and young, black and white, rich and poor, each ready to

do her part in the coming of the happy end"[25]—a new era of social justice.[26] The deferential hierarchy of the heterosexual family is supplanted
by the perfect equality of "sisters" bound together not by ties of kinship
but by their common vision of a community in which differences of age,
class, race, and personal history are mediated by gender, and in which
gender, in turn, is superseded by political commitment.

Unlike the all-white, all-male community with its unspoken commitment to the social reproduction of the middle class that Ragged Dick
discovers, the loving league of sisters dedicated to the obliteration of social inequality that Christie Devon labors to build acknowledges, by its
very composition, the differentials of class and race. Moreover, its figuring
of female alliance across the divides of race and class constitutes an argument for the contingent nature of those differences. Of necessity, the critical distinctions of class that are dissolved in Ragged Dick into the amor-
phous categories of poverty and prosperity, rags and respectability, are
finely detailed in Work. This difference in the communities Dick and
Christie inhabit is reinforced by the different means and ends of the narratives in which they figure. Whereas in Ragged Dick the route to success
is mapped by the charitable interventions of individual "gentlemen" on
behalf of boys who remind them of nothing so much as themselves, the
route to social equality requires, as Alcott's title suggests, work—not just
participation in waged work but, equally, participation in the special
work of reform for which experience of the inequities of gender, race, and
class that corrupt the workplace peculiarly prepares the model woman.
Yet despite the wide differences between these two narratives, their con-
vergence on the same-sex household and the domestic setting serves a
common function, for it is through the constitution of new kinds of homes
that both Ragged Dick and Work recuperate a vision of class harmony.

In spite of its feminist beginning and its final call to social action, that
is to say, the pivotal issue in Work is, yet again, securing a proper home
for the orphan. The novel's turning point comes in the tenth of its twenty
chapters when its protagonist arrives, on an April day, at an "old-fashioned cottage . . . in the midst of a garden" (220), a cottage that will
become not only her spiritual home but also her legal one and will, what is
more, provide her with the work for "hand and heart" she seeks. Entitled
"Beginning Again," this chapter introduces Christie and the reader into
a world made new, a suburban utopia in which the boundaries between
workplace and home, labor and pleasure, city and country are dissolved,
where economic sufficiency is achieved without competition or miserli-
ness and family extends beyond kinship to encompass "friends" in need.
A "half-way house," the cottage offers refuge to working women like
Christie who are in danger of being lost "for want of a home" (162). But

more than that, it offers a new-made, politically charged domesticity that answers the conflicted relationships of class, gender, race, and generation detailed in the first half of the novel.

In order to begin "again," however, Alcott must first begin. Taking up the story of the orphan girl at just the point where that story ordinarily concludes—that is, on the brink of marriage and adulthood—*Work* opens with Christie's announcement of a "new Declaration of Independence" (1). No ragged street urchin but a twenty-one-year-old "New England girl" of the Phoebe Pyncheon variety, Christie has long since been rescued from the trials of orphanhood by her mercenary farmer-uncle and his wife. Arriving at her majority, she rejects the limited prospects of the rural life into which she has been adopted—loveless marriage to a "bluff" young farmer "whose soul was wrapped up in prize cattle and big turnips" (12), embittered spinsterhood as a district schoolteacher, or suicide. "Hungry for love and a larger, nobler life" (12), "discontented, proud and ambitious," she does not intend "to sit and wait for any man to give [her] independence, if [she] can earn it [herself]" (8), but is instead determined to strike out on her own. Claiming her rights as an American and her equality as a woman, Christie sets out to make her way in the city like any promising New England boy.[27]

But herein, of course, lies the problem. For the story into which Christie expects to be catapulted by her brave decision to leave the farm—the story in which "people . . . travel away into the world and seek [their] fortune"—is, on the one hand, a boy's story and, on the other, a "fairy tale" (2). From the outset, that is to say, we have reason to anticipate the failure of Christie's venture. Not that we doubt that she possesses the promise, the energy, or the ambition necessary to success or believe that she must fail simply because she is a woman in a man's world. On the contrary, our doubts are aroused by the *kind* of woman Christie appears to be, a woman whose inborn gentility, whose "native refinement," must stand as an obstacle to her efforts to live the autonomous life reserved for men.

Yet another product of interclass marriage like Gerty Flint or Phoebe Pyncheon, Christie is the daughter of an impoverished gentleman and a restless country girl who, like herself, could not bear "the commonplace life" of her rural family. Christie has inherited her father's "refined tastes" along with his library, and her superiority to her countrified relatives is marked by her earnestness and, more conspicuously, by her perfect diction. "Rich in self-knowledge, self-control, and self-trust" (11), a "gentlewoman" who never "forgot the modesty of nature" (46, 48), Christie is determined to prove herself independent, and her consummate respectability and, less emphatically, her race lead her to expect the expanded opportunities of the city to satisfy her inchoate ambitions.

From the first, however, Christie is thwarted by her commitment to class- and race-based standards of femininity. The respectability to which Ragged Dick aspires and on which he rests his hopes for advancement constitutes, in its feminine form, not capital but liability. The very qualities Christie naively regards as her stock-in-trade—sensibility, refinement, and modesty—turn out to be worth less in the city than the "little suthing" her uncle gives her when she departs. Moreover, her understanding of her social position—an understanding framed by middle-class ideas of female respectability, white privilege, and American citizenship—is of little consequence in the world of waged work. Determined, however, to "Begin at the beginning, and work [her] way up" (16) like any aspiring boy, Christie discovers that the "beginning" is not where she had imagined it.

If Ragged Dick is destined, from the start, to be lifted out of the promiscuous community of Irish and native-born street urchins, Christie, if she is ultimately to mediate across the boundaries of social difference, must be brought down—brought, that is, into contact with working women whose respectability may be in doubt for reasons of race, nationality, or life experience, but whose womanly virtues are intact. Undaunted when her lack of accomplishment in the "ornamental" branches of education unexpectedly disqualifies her as a governess, the native-born Christie stalwartly joins the ranks of immigrant women seeking domestic service at "that purgatory of the poor, the intelligence office" (16).[28]

Not only do the benevolent gentlemen who appear with such convenient regularity to help Ragged Dick on his way have no female counterpart in *Work*, but Christie's work experiences demonstrate over and over the painful compromises to genteel femininity entailed by self-sufficiency. But if self-sufficiency is compromising, it is also instructive, as we learn in the first and framing episode of Christie's work life. Right from the start, she learns not, like Dick, of the interest her social "betters" might take in her but of the profound lack of interest prosperous women take in their "girls." The extent of this disinterest is made clear when the wealthy Mrs. Stuart, whose servant she becomes, insists that Christie be called Jane, the name to which Mrs. Stuart is "accustomed," a name that is putatively—but not actually, as we learn—the name of Christie's predecessor. This early lesson in the depersonalizing effects of waged work is followed by others more crucial which, taken together, initiate a process of moral and political revaluation that parallels—though it in no detail resembles—Ragged Dick's recalculation of his economic future. While Dick's new calculus brings him ever closer to the prosperous world inhabited by men for whom profit and charity go hand in hand, Christie's moral reckoning leads her to repudiate a world of wealth that presents itself to her as frivolous and uncaring.

Yearning for the place in cultivated society to which her paternity seems to entitle her, Christie is at first drawn to the "polite world" of the Stuarts. Assuming the part of the anonymous servant, she studies the rich and the famous, "laugh[s] at the wits, stare[s] at the lions, hear[s] the music" through a crack in the parlor door, and is "much edified by the gentility of the whole affair" (27). But that edification leads not to admiration or emulation but to repugnance. The "elegant sameness" of the "trained canaries" who attend the socially aspiring Stuarts' "evenings" soon bores her, and their "twaddle" about "art, and music, and poetry, and cosmos" quickly comes to seem artificial. In a city full of "appeals for help for the poor, and reforms of all kinds," their "dilettantism" comes to seem trivial and the fastidious gentility that prevents them from mentioning the pressing social issues of the day morally abhorrent. Exchanging "high" society for "low," renouncing art for truth, Christie rejects the pretentious "Society" of the eminently respectable Stuarts and embraces instead the society of their black cook, Hepsey.

The significance of this shift from parlor to kitchen as the site of value is consolidated in a single formative incident in which the refined Christie discovers, all at once, the combined impact of class, color, and gender. Having "just assumed her badge of servitude" (21), the white apron of the maid, she is summoned by a rain-drenched and impatient Mr. Stuart to remove and black his boots. Enraged at this utter disregard of her femininity and, it should be noted, her color, she expostulates to Hepsey: "It isn't the work; its the degradation, and I won't submit to it" (22). What is most obviously degrading in Mr. Stuart's demand is the requirement that Christie do the dirty work ordinarily—and rightfully, in her view—done by a boy—or a "boy." But compounding this violation of the gendered division of labor is Christie's dawning realization that, in the eyes of her employers, she is, first, a servant and only incidentally a woman. The refined sensibilities and cultivated tastes that she understands to define her femininity and that ought, she believes, in a democracy, to mark her as the Stuarts' equal are overridden by her new position in class.

Hepsey's response to this outburst simultaneously corroborates, complicates, and corrects Christie's understanding of her altered status. Hepsey concedes the slight to Christie's feelings as a woman—"I'se shore I'd never ask it of any woman if I was a man" (22)—but her understanding of that slight is framed by her experience of the more extreme system of oppression founded in race. "Quietly" recalling Christie to the fact that she is at least paid for her labor, the ex-slave Hepsey suggests that degradation is relative: "Dis ain't no deggydation to me now," she explains, "I's

a free woman" (22). But if the freedom of the wage makes blacking boots
no degradation to Hepsey, the blackness of her hands likewise ensures
that bootblacking can do her "ole hands no hurt" (22). This juxtaposition
of freedom and blackness, while it works to sever the connection between
race and slavery, also suggests the ways in which race is made to outweigh
gender for black women in a racist society.

Hepsey's allusion to the "greatest of all wrongs" puts Christie to
shame, diminishing the degradation of bootblacking to a "small injury"
(23) and reconciling her to her "servitude." But it also "bring[s] home to
her a sense of obligation so forcibly" that she begins at once "to pay a
little part of the great debt which the white race owes the black" (29).
The contrast between chattel slavery and waged work that makes Christie
grateful for her relatively luxurious position as a paid servant in a well-
appointed home, that is, also heightens her consciousness of the social
extremes embraced within the Stuart household and prompts her to action. The contrast between the slavery that has kept Hepsey illiterate and
the wealth that brings the literati to Mrs. Stuart's soirees leads Christie to
undertake Hepsey's education. Whereas Ragged Dick and Fosdick merge
their capital in a bargain destined to advance their individual social and
economic interests, Christie and Hepsey, united by shared gender oppression and racial guilt, join in an idealistic project of self-improvement.
While Hepsey learns to read, Christie, confronted with the advantages
that accrue to whiteness, learns the bitter lessons of inequality.

Unlike in *Ragged Dick*, where waged work and male respectability invariably go hand in hand, in *Work* the demands of work and womanhood
are chronically at odds. The first phase of Christie's working life predicts
what will follow. As she moves from job to job the insults to her refined
femininity multiply, and with each demonstration of that refinement her
isolation increases. Dismissed by the Stuarts because she is "too fond of
books" (33),[29] Christie takes a job as an actress. Forced to parry the sexual
advances of the stage manager but seduced by the "sound of applause,"
she realizes that she is a "fine actress" but worries about "how good a
woman" (51). Abandoning the "counterfeit" life of the stage, she takes a
post as a governess only to be pursued by the foppish brother of her
wealthy employer, who tries to blackmail her into marriage by threatening
to expose her disreputable career on the stage. Hired next to care for a
young woman suffering from hereditary insanity, she is lavishly paid and
satisfied that she is "doing good, as women best love to do it," but as a
menial employee she is deprived of the intimate facts of family history
that might allow her to prevent her patient's suicide. Nevertheless, having
dutifully begun at the beginning, up to this point Christie seems to garner
the rewards the workplace offers the industrious worker—not, as she had
hoped, autonomy, adventure, love, or nobility, but economic self-suffi-

ciency and the private pleasure of a job well done. On the death of her melancholy charge, however, Christie experiences "a great repugnance to . . . any place where she would be mixed up with family affairs again" (128). Leaving the remunerative world of private employment, she turns to sewing, the one form of work she has resolved "not to try till everything else failed" (16).

As a servant, Christie finds affection in Hepsey and womanly satisfaction in the proper care of the Stuarts' handsome rooms. As an actress, she is gratified by her success even as she is appalled by its cost to her modesty. As a governess, she is content with the progress of her young charges and flattered as well as enraged by Mr. Fletcher's romantic attentions. As a companion, her feminine sympathy has free rein and is rewarded with gratitude as well as money. But in Mrs. King's "well-conducted" mantua-making "establishment," Christie is reduced to "a sort of sewing-machine" (130).

Having first allied herself by proximity with unemployed immigrants and then by affection with an African American cook, the genteel Christie finally casts her lot with the proletariat of a sort. Seeking an antidote to the emotional entanglements of "family affairs," she finds respite in the laborious and repetitive task of assembling garments and diversion in the "fantasies of fashion" (129) produced in the factory-like workshop. But she finds too the profit-driven arrangements of the industrial workplace, where the demands of production and the reputation of the firm dictate not only continual surveillance of the women at work but intrusion into their private affairs, where the charitable interest of the employer in his employee so noteworthy in *Ragged Dick* is entirely superseded by concern with the bottom line, and where, for all its emphasis on respectability, the moral and social values of the model woman are unalterably pitted against the exigencies of waged work.

Not surprisingly, it is in the context of the mantua-making shop that the boy's plot collapses. Having chosen work over home—directly, when she leaves her uncle's house, and less directly, when she leaves domestic employment—Christie discovers that she has chosen wrongly, but not before trying to follow her decision to what would, in the case of a Ragged Dick, be its logical and satisfactory conclusion. In the stultifying tedium of the workshop, surrounded by sewing girls whose only "topics" are "dress, gossip, and wages" (129) and whose value to their employer is calculated exclusively in dollars and cents, Christie finds her Fosdick, the "friend" with whom she longs to share a home.

But the same-sex household that is constituted so easily in *Ragged Dick* is fraught with difficulty from the start in *Work*. The object of Christie's affection is a girl whose "haunting eyes" appeal to her with "mute eloquence" from across the workroom, a "creature sadder and more solitary than herself" but every bit as well-spoken, on whom she wants only to

whose needs money could supply" (148), she finds herself eventually alone, ill, in debt, and deeply embittered. But as the narrator makes clear, Christie's plight is not hers alone. Interrupting her story, she draws the lesson in the complexities of class directly. Christie is "no pauper"; she could, were she less committed to proving her self-sufficiency, call upon her uncle or her friends for aid. Instead, determined "to paddle [her] own canoe" as long as she can, she becomes "one of those whom poverty sets at odds with the world" (148). "Sad, bitter . . . rebellious" (148), she sees the "sharpness of the contrast" (156) between her condition and that of other women. Despite Christie's rebellious feelings, however, her recognition of the gulf dividing an impoverished working class from the possessors of wealth does not produce class consciousness, much less class struggle; rather, it simply compounds the problem of her individual position. For Christie, however "willing to work," is, we are reminded, one of many "poor gentlewomen" "unable to bear the contact with coarser natures which makes labor seem degrading" (149). Her like are urged by the more prosperous "to go into factories, or scrub in kitchens, for there is work enough for all," to which, the narrator observes, "the most convincing answer would be, 'Try it' " (149).

Christie's native gentility, her perfect middle-classness, that is to say, blocks the possibility of her proletarianization, despite the nature of her employment. Moreover, it translates what might be understood as an incipient and potentially dangerous awareness of the inequities of class, as well as of gender and race, into discontent of a different kind altogether. What Christie envies is, emphatically, not the wealth of other women but their "friends or lovers," their "home-love and happiness." As she contemplates bringing the "long, lonely years before her" to an end, we are reminded that "It is not always want, insanity, or sin that drives women to desperate deaths; often it is a dreadful loneliness of heart, a hunger for home" (150). Set in the context of Christie's "waiting, hoping, longing for her friend," her "fervently made nightly prayer" (142) for Rachel's return, Christie's bitter rebelliousness is stripped of its political import at the same time that it signals ever more clearly the problem of the same-sex couple.

In the grip of despair, with neither friend nor work, dunned by her landlady and unwilling to ask for help, Christie wanders the city streets, coming to rest, exhausted and ill, on a wharf by the river. There she is transfixed by the image of herself in the water, but unlike Narcissus, what she sees is not the tantalizing image of her own beauty but rather her drowned self: "So plainly did she see it, so peaceful was the white face, so full of rest the folded hands, so strangely like, and yet unlike herself, that she seemed to lose her identity" (158). But just as "some blind impulse" propels her toward union with her drowned double, a woman's

hand seizes her and she is "herself again." The woman is, of course, Rachel. The narcissistic image of her dead self is replaced, quite implausibly,
by the no less narcissistic image of her twin, the "sister" who will, before
the novel is done, become her sister-in-law and whose history, barring her
one misstep, parallels Christie's. In view of modern literary representations of homosexuality, it is difficult not to read this invocation of narcissistic union and of the potentially fatal effects of same-sex coupling as a
sign of sexual danger.[31] "Gathered close to Rachel's heart" (160), Christie
is saved not only from death but also, as it turns out, from homosexuality.

Like Ragged Dick, Christie ultimately finds a way of fusing home and
work, the affectional and the economic, but in her case this requires step-
ping outside the workplace, not into it, and making common cause with
the oppressed, not rising above them. Having lost everything on account
of her love for Rachel, Christie turns to Rachel in her moment of need,
and Rachel immediately sets about restoring in more perfect form what
has been lost. In lieu of the home with Rachel for which she longed and
the work she needed, Christie finds, through Rachel's agency, refuge and
a calling with the mother and brother who rejected Rachel for her sin.
Taken in by the Sterlings, "not as a servant" but, crucially, as a "helper"
(211), she "begins again" in a place as yet unimagined in the novel. Posi-
tioned midway between the city and the rural backwater she has fled, the
Sterling cottage occupies a middle ground geographically and represents
as well a golden mean socially. No "gilded cage," neither is the Sterling
house filled with the rambunctious children and steaming laundry coppers
Christie has encountered in the home of the working-class Wilkinses.

But if the "old-fashioned" domestic arrangements, the grace and simplicity, of the Sterling household answer the superficiality of the wealthy,
the disorder of the poor, and the moral vacuousness of a money-grubbing
middle class, so too do its economic arrangements answer the heart-
lessness of waged work. David Sterling supports the household as a nurs-
eryman, a form of work that not only renders him independent of the
corrupt relationships of the market—his greenhouses are, literally, at
home—but also allies him with the natural world. The flowers he grows
are "not merely valued . . . as merchandise" but known and loved as
"friends" (236). And "friends"—in particular, the desperate young working women like Christie who take refuge at the Sterlings—are tended as
carefully as the most delicate blossom.

Ensconced in a room "as plain and white and still as a nun's cell" (221),
Christie finds her perfect setting in the Sterling cottage, but she has yet to
find her ideal role. Committed to the equation of singleness (or single-
sexedness) with independence, she prefers single carnations to the "un-
tidy" double ones, having yet to learn that the former are "seldom perfect,

and look . . . incomplete" (255). Returned to the girl's proper setting, a home of the very best kind, and to the girl's narrative, she must, as the flowery language that dominates her attenuated romance with David Sterling suggests, leave her "nun's cell" and marry.

Marriage, however, rather than being the endpoint in Alcott's narrative, is instead an instrumental stage in the production of female community. Having been brought to the brink of suicide by the combined effects of despair at her loss of Rachel and the impossibility of fulfilling simultaneously the roles of womanly woman and independent worker, Christie must, if she is to model a new and improved femininity, step outside of the world of waged work and be returned as well to heterosexuality. In an inversion of the pattern whereby a woman serves as the conduit for men's mutual interest in one another, the love between Christie and Rachel is negotiated through and deflected toward Rachel's brother. But if Christie's marriage to David solves the problem of the same-sex couple, it also solves the problem of female independence. David is not Christie's "lord and master," nor she his household drudge. As if to ensure this point, immediately upon marrying they leave the peaceful cottage to join the "rich and poor" who have proved "that they [love] their liberty better than their money or their lives" (359) by enlisting in the Union army. "Shoulder to shoulder," the "faithful comrades" march off to the Civil War, one as soldier, the other as nurse. Having "always wanted to . . . have a part in great deeds" (376), Christie finally gets romance and adventure, love and heroism, all at once.

What she does not get, perhaps because Alcott found it unrepresentable or more likely because it is incidental to her purposes, is a domestic life with David, a life that would have to live up to the ideal of companionate marriage. Instead, David conveniently dies while rescuing a bereaved slave mother, and Christie returns, pregnant with a daughter, to inherit cottage and nursery and to take up life with Mrs. Sterling and her daughter, the long-lost Rachel. Finding consolation and new purpose in her child, she takes "garden and green-house into her own hands," taking in several young women to help her, and reorganizes life in the cottage along communitarian lines. As she explains to her uncle, who is contemplating the disposition of his "hoard," the women "work for one another and share everything together": unlike Dick and Fosdick, they "don't make bargains" (419).

Having proven her femininity and gotten her Rachel as well, and having inherited a home to boot, Christie finds at last "the task [her] life has been fitting her for," a "new field of labor" that simultaneously exploits "all the lessons of her life" (428) and ratifies her womanhood. A "genuine woman"—wife, mother, and widow—and "a working-woman," a "sister" offering not pity but "justice as a right" (429), drawing on the "fine instincts" and "gracious manners" of her gentleman father as well as her mother's "practical virtues" and "love of independence" (430), Christie sets out to "lay the foundation of a new emancipation" (431), the emancipation of working women from oppression, wealthy ones from frivolity, and all of them from dependence. Deeming herself "a radical, and a reformer," "having done all sorts of dreadful things to get [a] living" and having "neither youth, beauty, talent, or position" (437) but only conviction, Christie discovers her true calling as an "interpreter between the two classes" (430).

Attending a meeting of women "workers" and the "ladies" who would be their allies, Christie is seized by a "sudden and uncontrollable impulse" (427) to address the crowd. Identifying herself neither as "worker" nor "lady" but instead as a "working-woman," her "magical" speech, in which, we are assured, there is "no learning, no statistics, and no politics" (429), asserts her rightful position as intermediary. Capturing in her very syntax, as it were, the experiences of all women, Christie, like her antecedents in midcentury fiction, displays the unique social competence of the white middle-class woman. Eluding the strictures of class by assimilating all class experience to herself, she embodies the prospect of class harmony even as she demands justice for those disabled by class. Like her home, the spotless simplicity of which makes no claim to social superiority, the suburban location of which unites work and domesticity, and the habitués of which include all colors, conditions, and ages, if not all sexes, the omnifarious Christie "bridge[s]" all the "space[s] that . . . divide" (430). True to her name, she emerges at the close of the novel as the perfect "mediator," a figure belonging to every class by dint of belonging to none, whose perfect womanliness, refined and independent, and whose perfect setting, both workplace and home, promises harmony and justice alike.

EPILOGUE

The fictional home in which inequalities are erased and class struggle averted, in which the circle of "friends" includes millions and mills, blacks and whites, in which homosociality enables cross-class sociability, is designed to answer the demands of social justice and the fears of social conflict alike. A projection in literary space of the woman whose ideal middle-classness is signified by her claim to a self outside of class, this home of the better sort, as I have suggested, lies outside of history, but also, of course, in it. For the syntax that links the many forms of home and the problem of class is not exclusively literary, nor is harmony always its meaning. In closing this study, I want to suggest that real historical actors for whom home was a sign of citizenship and a site of conflict ordered and reordered the syntax of class to make meanings of their own.

In the spring of 1869, a group of workers and ladies remarkably like the one conjured up in Alcott's *Work* met in Boston to discuss a petition urging the Massachusetts legislature to assist in financing housing for working women. The *Workingman's Advocate*, one of the most influential labor newspapers of the day, covered the proceedings of this gathering in an article titled "THE WORKING WOMEN. White Slavery in New England," paying particular attention to the opening address given by one "Miss Phelps." The impassioned plea made by Miss Phelps—"no speechmaker—only a worker"[1]—on behalf of the pieceworkers, "tailoresses," and paper-box makers of Boston stands in sharp contrast to the one Alcott imagines. Miss Phelps draws, no less than the novelists this study has considered, on the syntax of workers and "women," of orphans and daughters, of citizens and slaves, of male and female, black and white. But unlike those writers, she turns to the state—not "charitable institutions," not Perley Kelso or Christie Devon, but legislators and "the people"—to "give these women little homes" (107).

Claiming the right of every woman to a home of her own, not "a husband's or a father's," Miss Phelps speaks as a worker and, like Alcott, as a feminist. But she anticipates neither the moral nor the social regeneration of her class. Granting working women homes will not, she insists, transform workers into "women"; it will not bring them into conformity with the ethical or the behavioral specifications of the middle class. But respectable or not, the uneducated, the "improvident and shiftless" (107), the physically weak, and the thoroughly deskilled women earning twenty-five cents a day in Boston's sweatshops "love independence" (108) as much as any Christie Devon, and justice demands that they be allowed to achieve it. Their homelessness, after all, is no accident; it is the by-product of an industrial "system which makes women homeless," a system of sweated labor wherein "one . . . makes the button-holes, and another puts the buttons on, and when the poor girl . . . finds her work slack she goes from shop to shop, perhaps for weeks, before she can find the same kind of work" (107). No fault of "individuals," this system relies on a class segregation that keeps the "men of Massachusetts" and the ladies whose "every costly dress . . . makes three prostitutes" (108) ignorant of the cost in "homelessness" of the luxuries they consume. That the working women of Boston "feel the difference between their condition and that of . . . ladies" she leaves no doubt. Offering no assurance of social harmony, she claims the right of the worker to a home, not as the expression of a feminine social virtue or as the object of masculine speculative investment, but as a place to live, neither as hapless orphan nor as proletarianized "slave," but as citizen. For to be without a home in America, Miss Phelps understands, is to be without "a country."

The reforming middle class, with its deep fear of class conflict, its obsessive concern with self-control, and its devotion to "home—in the better sense" as a figure of social harmony, shaped, in large measure, the literary syntax of class in mid-nineteenth-century America. The illusion that homes—in the better sense—would make the homeless just like them and thus obviate class antagonism required the particular compound of obliviousness and arrogance characteristic of a middle-class that believed their way of living was not simply theirs but right. For others, less favored, home was neither a symbolic site in which competing interests might be harmonized nor the site of initiation into the ways of the respectable. Rather, then as now, home was itself a locus of conflict, a thing to be struggled over and for.

NOTES

Introduction

1. Francis Bowen, " 'Phillips' Protection and Free Trade," *North American Review* 72 (1851): 415. Quoted in Martin J. Burke, *The Conundrum of Class: Public Discourse on the Social Order in America* (Chicago: University of Chicago Press, 1995), 120.

2. The February 1848 overthrow of Louis Phillipe, imagined at first by Americans as the fulfillment of their own republican revolution, was met in the United States with torchlight parades, fireworks, speeches, poems, song, and celebration. By March, Horace Greeley's *New York Tribune* was proclaiming the fall of the French monarch to be the beginning of the "Emancipation of Europe" from despotism. With the much-admired Lamartine apparently in control of events in France and political uprisings spreading across Europe, the *Tribune*'s optimism seemed warranted. By July, however, the *Tribune* was less sanguine. Writing from France after the violence of the June Days, former city editor and Brook Farmer Charles A. Dana reported that Lamartine, though "a man of noble aspiration," was unequal to "the great practical work" (quoted in Larry J. Reynolds, *European Revolutions and the American Literary Renaissance* [New Haven: Yale University Press, 1988], 48) of the social revolution now sweeping France and much of the rest of Europe. Like the Chartists who had been dispersed by the military in London in April, the French workers who took to the barricades in June wanted not only political change but social change as well. Despite alarming headlines like that of the *New York Courier and Enquirer*—"Communism, Socialism, Pillage, Murder, Anarchy, the Guillotine vs. Law and Order, Family and Property" (ibid., 45)—Dana insisted that the Parisian workers were neither communists nor socialists. Rather, they cherished "a conviction, which they carry to fanaticism, that justice is and cannot be done by the existing relation of employed and employer" (ibid., 48). As the demands of European workers grew louder, the bitterness of class animosity more apparent, and state repression more violent, Americans despaired of European republicanism and the radicals of 1848 were denounced as heirs not to the American Revolution but to the French. The lesson of 1848 was, it seemed, that "Republics," as the conservative publisher George Ticknor announced with finality, "cannot grow on the soil of Europe" (ibid., 15). As well-to-do Americans watched fearfully, French insurgents and British Chartists enacted their worst nightmares of working-class rebellion. New York, according to editor Evert Duykinck, was filled with "recollections of Robespierre" (ibid., 10), and the historian George Bancroft reported that genteel Boston was "frightened out of its wits" (ibid., 8).

3. Quoted in Karen Halttunen, *Confidence Men and Painted Women* (New Haven: Yale University Press, 1982), 195.

4. *Account of the Terrific and Fatal Riot at the New-York Astor Place Opera House* (New York: H. M. Ranney, 1849; reprint, New York: Museum of the City of New York, 1999), 19, 32.

5. George Foster, *New York by Gaslight*, ed. Stuart M. Blumin (Berkeley: University of California Press, 1990), 69.

6. Quoted in Paul Boyer, *Urban Masses and Moral Order in America, 1820–1920* (Cambridge: Harvard University Press, 1978), 80.

7. Ibid.

8. Lydia Maria Child, *Letters from New York* (Freeport: Books for Libraries Press, 1970), 13.

9. Elizabeth Stuart Phelps, *The Silent Partner* (1871; Old Westbury, N.Y.: Feminist Press, 1983), 295.

10. I allude here to Michael Denning's discussion in *Mechanic Accents: Dime Novels and Working-Class Culture in America* (New York: Verso, 1987) of the "ruse of class representation." Following Marx, Denning argues that historical struggles are played out in masquerade and, further, that the conventional characters that inhabit popular fiction are one source for the disguises necessary to that masquerade. Writing from the point of view of a particular group of actors in those historical struggles, namely the working-class reader of the dime novel, Denning contends that insofar as these conventional characters offer a "body of representations . . . alternatively claimed, rejected, and fought over" (77) they provide a vehicle for the playing out of class difference.

11. See Gareth Stedman-Jones, *Languages of Class: Studies in English Working-Class History, 1832–1982* (New York: Cambridge University Press, 1983), introduction.

12. See Sherry B. Ortner, "Reading America: Preliminary Notes on Class and Culture," in *Recapturing Anthropology: Working in the Present*, ed. Richard Fox (Santa Fe: American Research Press, 1991), 163–87. Writing about twentieth-century America, Ortner contends that if modern Americans can be said to have a discourse of class at all, that discourse is a wholly economistic one—a discourse, as she puts it, of money. Her useful discussion of the displacement of class—and more particularly, of class friction—into the languages of race, ethnicity, and gender not only highlights, as she notes, a deep cultural commitment to the tenets of liberal individualism but points to the distortions and antagonisms that this displacement produces in sexual and racial relations.

13. For an explanation of "class-defeating" identities, see Stuart M. Blumin, *The Emergence of the Middle Class* (New York: Cambridge University Press, 1989), 250.

14. See Cora Kaplan, "Millennial Class," *PMLA* 115 (2000): 13.

15. In slightly different forms, this argument appears in my essay "The Syntax of Class in Elizabeth Stuart Phelps's *The Silent Partner*" (267–85) and in Michael T. Gilmore and Wai Chee Dimock's introduction (1–11) to *Rethinking Class*, ed. Gilmore and Dimock (New York: Columbia University Press, 1994).

16. From Georg Lukács to Ian Watt and, more recently, Michael McKeon, Benedict Anderson, and D. A. Miller, the ideological work of the novel—particularly but not exclusively the English novel—in producing or expressing the hegemony of the middle classes, in debating or policing the instabilities of the social

order, and in constituting the modern nation has absorbed the interest of genera-tions of literary scholars. More recently, feminist scholarship, postcolonial stud-ies, and diasporic studies have both challenged and vastly complicated the read-ings of class in the novel. With notable exceptions like the work of Myra Jehlen, Michael T. Gilmore, and Wai Chee Dimock, class has figured less prominently than gender and race in scholarly discussion of American literature over the past quarter century.

17. Stuart M. Blumin provides a neat synopsis of the "consensus" narrative of middle-class formation in "The Hypothesis of Middle-Class Formation in Nine-teenth-Century America: A Critique and Some Proposals," *American Historical Review* 90 (1985): 299–338.

In the United States, according to this view, the culture that in Europe was associated with a particular class (located hierarchically between a formally aristo-cratic upper class and a decidedly plebeian lower class) broke out of its class boundaries to provide a common system of belief and action and a powerful source of national cohesion. Hence middle-class formation is best seen not as a type or aspect of class formation but as the development of bourgeois liberalism within the culture as a whole (302).

18. I use the term "self-awareness" here to allude to the distinction between class awareness and class consciousness drawn by Anthony Giddens. This distinc-tion is further elaborated in chapter I.

19. Blumin, "Hypothesis," 305, 309.

20. E. P. Thompson's critical redefinition of class in *The Making of the English Working Class* (New York: Vintage, 1966) as both fluid and relational—as a pro-cess that "evades analysis if we attempt to stop it dead at any given moment and anatomise its structure" and, moreover, as a historical relationship that must be "embodied in real people in a real context" (9)—has been of enormous impor-tance to literary scholarship on class. This is not least because, while founded in productive relations, class is, for Thompson, both made and made manifest in the whole array of cultural productions, including those that stand at a distance from the workplace (that site notoriously absent from nineteenth-century American fiction). But beyond this, Thompson's view of class is peculiarly resonant for the literary scholar, because if thinking about class entails thinking about historical relationships, so too does thinking about novels. "We cannot," as Thompson puts it, "have two distinct classes, each with an independent being, and then bring them *into* relationship with each other. We cannot have love without lovers, nor deference without squires and laborers" (9)—except perhaps in the novel, where, with characters already marked as lovers or squires, workers or owners, class "happens" as they are brought into relationship with one another.

21. Carolyn Kay Steedman, *Landscape for a Good Woman* (New Brunswick, N.J.: Rutgers University Press, 1987), 14.

22. This predominance of gender as an analytic category has broken down more readily in the recent study of working-class women from Christine Stansell's *City of Women* to Kathy Peiss's *Cheap Amusements* to Nan Enstad's just-pub-lished *Ladies of Labor, Girls of Adventure*. Nonetheless, it has been overwhelm-ingly the case that class has provided the analytic frame for the historical account

of middle-class men in the nineteenth-century United States, while gender has provided the frame for accounts of women.

23. Blumin, *Emergence of the Middle Class*, 248–49.

CHAPTER I

1. Quoted in Christine Stansell, *City of Women: Sex and Class in New York, 1789–1860* (Chicago: University of Illinois, 1987), 194.

2. Charles Loring Brace, *The Dangerous Classes of New York, and Twenty Years' Work among Them* (New York: Wynkoop and Hallenbeck, 1880; reprint, Montclair, N.J.: Patterson Smith, 1967), 29, 317.

3. For a discussion of changing definitions of theft in this period, see Stansell, *City of Women*, 203–9.

4. Ibid., 195, 202.

5. Ibid., 202.

6. Ibid.

7. Susan Warner, *The Wide, Wide World* (New York: Feminist Press, 1997), 41.

8. Ibid., 64.

9. In other novels, such as Elizabeth Stuart Phelps's enormously popular post–Civil War novel of spiritual consolation, *The Gates Ajar*, the boundary between heaven and home is all but obliterated.

10. See Richard Brodhead, *Cultures of Letters* (Chicago: University of Chicago Press, 1993), chapter 1.

11. Stansell, *City of Women*, 213.

12. Karen Halttunen, *Confidence Men and Painted Women* (New Haven: Yale University Press, 1982), 195.

13. Quoted in Stuart M. Blumin, *The Emergence of the Middle Class* (New York: Cambridge University Press, 1989), 10. For a discussion of Giddens's understanding of class and its relevance to the "elusive" American middle class, see Blumin's chapter 1.

14. It is worth noting here, as Lora Romero does in *Home Fronts: Domesticity and Its Critics in the Antebellum United States* (Durham, N.C.: Duke University Press, 1997), that the fact that "antebellum authors use gender difference to stabilize categorical distinctions" (9), including those of class, does not mean that some "essential and ineluctable political tendency" inheres within domestic fictions. On the contrary, as Romero suggests, it is far more useful to assume that "the politics of culture reside in local formulations—and in the social and historical locations of those formulations" (6–7).

15. Laura Wexler, "Tender Violence: Literary Eavesdropping, Domestic Fiction, and Educational Reform," in *The Culture of Sentiment: Race, Gender, and Sentimentality in Nineteenth-Century America*, ed. Shirley Samuels (New York: Oxford University Press, 1992), 15.

16. Mary P. Ryan, *Cradle of the Middle Class* (New York: Cambridge University Press, 1981), 240.

17. Of course, as Myra Jehlen, Nancy Cott, and others have demonstrated, the insularity, the "privacy," ascribed the middle-class home in literary culture is belied by its actual function in antebellum social and economic life.

18. My point is that as much as the middle-class woman's actual movement in the city, her sensibility—her reading of novels "with a purpose," as an 1874 *Harper's* article dubbed them; her devotion to charitable labor; the parlor display of sentimental engravings of the poor of the kind Hans Bergmann reports (see *God in the Street* [Philadelphia: Temple University Press, 1995], 103–4)—evinces her ability to traverse class.

19. Wexler, "Tender Violence," 17.

20. Maria Cummins, *The Lamplighter* (1854; New York: Odyssey Press, 1968), 213. Hereafter cited parenthetically in the text.

21. Confirming Gerty's likeness to Cinderella, Cummins makes parodic reference later in the novel to the fairy-tale rise of the orphan in the ashes when the wealthy Belle Clinton borrows Gerty's rubbers, only to discover, to her embarrassment, that her feet are far too large to fit them.

22. The term is Brodhead's in *Cultures of Letters*, chapter 1.

23. The phrase is Kathryn K. Sklar's in *Catherine Beecher: A Study in American Domesticity* (New York: Norton, 1973).

24. On the ritual significance of Gerty's tea-making in *The Wide, Wide World*, see Jane Tompkins, *Sensational Designs: The Cultural Work of American Fiction, 1790–1860* (New York: Oxford University Press, 1985), chapter 6.

25. This is not to slight the Christian significance of the play of light and dark in *The Lamplighter*: Emily is blind and can therefore "see"; Trueman Flint is associated with the heavenly "Lamplighter" who lights the stars and to whom Gerty appeals in her worst moments; enlightenment is throughout bound to the embrace of Christianity, darkness to ignorance of God's love. Nonetheless, in *The Lamplighter*, as opposed to the more doctrinaire *The Wide, Wide World*, Christianity is deployed to clear social ends. The dictates of Christianity facilitate and confirm but never supersede the demands of social harmony.

26. My point is that in Gerty, as in the working women in later industrial novels, "darkness" is bound to gender transgression as well as class origins. In fact, Gerty's temper appears by the end of the novel to be, in part, a patrilineal genetic trait, passed down from her father, Philip Amory.

27. See Wai Chee Dimock, *Empire for Liberty: Melville and the Poetics of Individualism* (Princeton: Princeton University Press, 1988), 197 ff.

28. Unlikely as this proximity may seem, it captures the class heterogeneity of urban neighborhoods in the antebellum Northeast documented by Blumin and others.

29. Nathaniel Hawthorne, *The House of the Seven Gables* (1851; Columbus: Ohio State University Press, 1965), 263. Hereafter cited parenthetically in the text.

30. T. Walter Herbert, *Dearest Beloved: The Hawthornes and the Making of the Middle Class* (Berkeley: University of California Press, 1993), chapter 6.

31. Possible resolutions of the conflict are figured—and thwarted—again and again in the novel. The crime for which Clifford Pyncheon goes to jail originates in the desire of his uncle, to restore the Maules' property and end the curse; simi-

larly, the exchange agreed upon by Gervayse Pyncheon and Matthew Maule generations previously is thwarted ultimately by their methods.

32. For a discussion of Dimmesdale and Chillingworth's relationship, see Romero, *Home Fronts*, chapter 5.

33. Eve Kosofsky Sedgwick, *Between Men: English Literature and Male Homosocial Desire* (New York: Columbia University Press, 1985), 25.

34. Teresa Goddu, "The Circulation of Women in *The House of the Seven Gables*," *Studies in the Novel* 22, no. 1 (1991): 119–27.

35. Nina Baym, *Novels, Readers, and Reviewers: Responses to Fiction in Antebellum America* (Ithaca: Cornell University Press, 1984), 210.

36. Quoted from *Tait's Edinburgh Magazine* in Milton R. Stern's introduction to Hawthorne's *The House of the Seven Gables* (New York: Viking Penguin, 1981), xxx.

37. For one reading of effortless labor in *Seven Gables*, see Gillian Brown, *Domestic Individualism: Imagining Self in Nineteenth-Century America* (Berkeley: University of California Press, 1990), chapter 3.

38. See Walter Benn Michaels, *The Gold Standard and the Logic of Naturalism* (Berkeley: University of California, 1987), 97, and Herbert, *Dearest Beloved*, 100.

39. Herbert, *Dearest Beloved*, 105.

CHAPTER II

1. This is not to say that the domestic novel—or those novels that, like *The House of the Seven Gables*, employ the conventions of domesticity—are invariably either conservative or subversive in their impulse, a question feminist literary critics from Myra Jehlen to Lora Romero have considered. My interest lies in the detailed working out of underlying assumptions about class and classlessness which, while at times relevant to the political valence of the novels under discussion here, are in no way predictive of it.

2. Unlike Rowland Berthoff, on whose "Conventional Mentality: Free Blacks, Women, and Business Corporations as Unequal Persons, 1820–1870" (*Journal of American History* 76 [December 1989]: 753–84) I rely here, my interest in these debates lies in their use of the language of social difference and, more particularly, in the recourse to the language of class in the defense of gender- and race-based exclusions. The focus of Berthoff's illuminating essay is, rather, on the historiographic problem of nineteenth-century liberalism and on the consistent and paradoxical willingness of the delegates to these conventions to deny constitutional rights to women and blacks while conferring "personhood" on corporations. Berthoff's article is hereafter cited parenthetically in the text.

3. Italics mine. Here, as in the literary version, the relationship between the "coarse," the non-"white," and the unfeminine is crucial.

4. For a discussion of the contemporary British reviews of *The Garies* as well as the best account to date of Webb's life, see Rosemary F. Crockett, "Frank J. Webb: The Shift to Color Discrimination," in *The Black Columbiad*, ed. Werner Sollers and Maria Diedrich (Cambridge: Harvard University Press, 1994). The extent of *The Garies*' readership is quite unclear. According to Crockett, George

Routledge & Company printed two thousand copies of the deluxe edition of the novel and twelve thousand less expensive copies, numbers suggesting that Routledge at least anticipated successful sales. A comment in the *New Era* in January 1870 claims that the book was indeed read both in the United States and in Britain, but evidence of the novel's popularity is thin.

5. In 1969, Arno Press and the *New York Times* briefly brought into print a paperback facsimile edition of *The Garies* as part of its series "The American Negro: His History and Literature." A second paperback edition, also a facsimile of the 1857 London edition, was published in 1997 by Johns Hopkins University Press. For most of the intervening years, *The Garies* was available (if at all) only in a costly library edition.

6. See Arthur P. Davis, "*The Garies and Their Friends*: A Neglected Pioneer Novel," *CLA Journal* 13, no. 1 (1969): 33, and James DeVries, "The Tradition of the Sentimental Novel in *The Garies and Their Friends*," *CLA Journal* 17, no. 2 (1973): 241.

7. See R. F. Bogardis, "Frank J. Webb's *The Garies and Their Friends*: An Early Black Novelist's Venture into Realism," *Studies in Black Literature* 5, no. 2 (1974): 15, 19.

8. Quoted in John Runcie, " 'Hunting the Nigs' in Philadelphia: The Race Riot of August, 1834," *Pennsylvania History* 39 (1972): 189.

9. Ibid., 190.

10. From 1815 until they were disenfranchised in 1838, free black men with property sufficient to meet the state's requirement had been eligible to vote in Pennsylvania. The same 1837 convention that denied African American men the ballot on the grounds of color extended the suffrage to include all white men over the age of twenty-one regardless of property.

11. Using census data from 1838 and 1856, Theodore Hershberg, in his "Free Blacks in Antebellum Philadelphia" (in *The Peoples of Philadelphia: A History of Ethnic Groups and Lower-Class Life*, ed. Allen F. Davis and Mark H. Heller [Philadelphia: Temple University Press, 1973], 111–33), argues that discrimination accounts for the dramatic lack of occupational differentiation among black Philadelphians in this period: eight out of ten black workingmen labored at unskilled jobs, while eight out of ten black workingwomen worked as domestic servants of one sort or another (124–5).

12. Following the work of George Rude and Charles Tilly on European urban mobs, Runcie raises and then distances himself from the argument that the rioters of 1834 "used violence in a rational, controlled way . . . in the attainment of specific goals" ("Hunting the Nigs," 207). Despite his conclusion that the 1834 mob, however purposeful, was neither tightly controlled nor unified in its motives, Runcie presents powerful evidence that its activities were not wholly spontaneous. In fact, he argues that the riot was instigated by powerful members of the white political and social elite. Not surprisingly, many contemporary observers believed it to have been the result of "a preconcerted organized plan" (208).

13. Ibid., 209.

14. Ibid., 215.

15. In his introduction to the second and most recent paperback reprinting of *The Garies and Their Friends* (Baltimore: Johns Hopkins University Press, 1997),

Robert Reid-Pharr uses somewhat different language to make a similar observation. Likewise disclaiming the usefulness of critical efforts to locate Webb's novel in either the sentimental or the realist camp, Reid-Pharr argues that Webb rejects the "very distinction between the domestic and the political" (xi). My preference for "home" and "history" as the terms in this discussion has to do with the fact that these seem to me to conjure up more fully Webb's allusive use of the larger ideological formation of nineteenth-century domesticity, his efforts to locate "home" in the history of black liberation—and, not incidentally, his detailed attention to real estate.

16. Claudia Tate, *Psychoanalysis and Black Novels: Desire and the Protocols of Race* (New York: Oxford University Press, 1998), 6.

17. Tate's account of the "protocols of black textuality" in *Psychoanalysis and Black Novels* has been of great assistance to my thinking both about *The Garies* and about the dismay expressed by critics like Arthur P. Davis at the "mildness" of Webb's "protest novel" and, more particularly, at its failure to launch a "frontal attack on slavery" ("*The Garies and Their Friends,*" 33, 31). Writing about modernist fiction, Tate explores the ways in which twentieth-century African American authors negotiated the tension between the deeply felt (and politically essential) imperative to tell and retell the stories of "unremitting racial trauma" (18)—the "manifest narrative" of black fiction—and another, equally powerful, need to recount the subjective experience of individual African Americans. According to Tate, what is generated out of that tension is a "surplus," a "textual enigma" that "disrupts the conscious plot about racial/social protest or affirmation" (13), which, insofar as it dominates the text, is taken to call into question its racial authenticity.

18. Tate, *Psychoanalysis and Black Novels*, 10.

19. Robert Reid-Pharr, introduction to Frank J. Webb, *The Garies and Their Friends* (1857; Baltimore: Johns Hopkins University Press, 1997), ix. This edition is hereafter cited parenthetically in the text.

20. Acknowledging the positions of blacks and whites relative to their racial communities, W.E.B. DuBois, in his exhaustive study of *The Philadelphia Negro* (1899; reprint, Philadelphia: University of Pennsylvania Press, 1996), identifies "the middle class of workers" as the "servant class. . . the best of the laborers" (317, 315).

21. Ibid., 317.

22. According to Noel Ignatiev, the riot in *The Garies and Their Friends* most closely resembles what is known as the California House riot of 1849. One of Philadelphia's bloodiest, this riot began with an election-eve attack on a tavern owned by a black man recently married to a white woman. In other respects, the riot Webb describes resembles the Flying Horse riot of 1834, in which the son of James Forten, Philadelphia's most prominent African American resident, was attacked. See Ignatiev, *How the Irish Became White* (New York: Routledge, 1995), 155–56, 125–30.

23. C.L.R. James, *The Black Jacobins* (New York: Random House, 1963), 19.

24. See Robert Bone's brief treatment of *The Garies* in *The Negro Novel in America* (New Haven: Yale University Press, 1965).

25. The confused response of Birdie's father to the revelation of Clarence's parentage, a response in which character and color are thoroughly intertwined,

is an index to the complexity of Webb's understanding of the (il)logic of racism. First furiously condemning Clarence as a "contemptible, *black-hearted* nigger" (352, my italics)—as if black heart and black skin were one and the same or, alternatively, entirely separable—Mr. Bates goes on to berate him as a "counterfeit," accusing Clarence of "palming" himself off on white society. Insisting that had Clarence "been unaware of his origins" he "would have deserved sympathy," but that for "acting a lie" he merits only "execration and contempt" (354), Mr. Bates seems momentarily to suggest that Clarence's duplicity and not his race is at issue. By the end of the exchange, however, the matter is clear: Birdie has been "wasting her affections upon a worthless nigger" (354).

26. The younger George Stevens, a "thoroughly spoiled and naturally evil-disposed boy" (128), grows up to be a thoroughly dissolute and equally evil-disposed man. Interested only in spending the fortune his father has so conveniently acquired through the Garies' murder, young George in effect commits a second murder when he exposes Clarence's racial origins to the family of his fiancée. His sister Lizzie, by contrast, is from the outset "sweetness itself" (127). On learning of her father's crime, she is stricken with guilt and urges him to make restitution to the Garie children, insisting that she would "rather work day and night . . . than ever touch a penny of the money thus accumulated" (358).

27. That the Irish are reluctant agents of violence—are, in fact, blackmailed into participating in the riot by Stevens—is evident from the story of the hapless McCloskey.

28. Runcie, "Hunting the Nigs," 206.

29. As with the original and final homes of Gerty and Willie, the proximity of mansion and slum attests to the incomplete class segregation of cities like Philadelphia and Boston, where homes of the better sort—even the best sort—often backed on alleys occupied by the working poor.

30. Embedded in the assumption of open mobility for whites that supports this belief is the danger of hypocrisy, a danger of which the urban white middle class was acutely conscious and of which Stevens is only the most dramatic example. Early in *The Garies*, Mrs. Ellis and her daughter Caddy take a walk that stands, in retrospect, as the obverse of Stevens's. Strolling through the "fashionable part of the city" (19), Mrs Ellis recounts the origins in trade of one after another of the "aristocratic" white residents of Chestnut Street. One palatial residence is inhabited by the grandson of a yeast-maker, another "splendid mansion" by the scion of an undertaker (20–21); yet another is occupied by the "fashionable descendant of the worthy maker of leathern britches" (67), and still others, we later learn, belong to "aristocrats" whose ancestry can be traced to "the cobbler's bench or the huckster's stall" (73). Fashionable Chestnut Street is, in fact, "a quarter into which many of its residents had retired, that they might be out of sight of the houses in which their fathers or grandfathers had made their fortunes" (20).

The pretense to aristocracy of the white hypocrites of Chestnut Street echoes and inverts Stevens's masquerade. From the perspective of a white middle class alarmed by an urban world of strangers, it illustrates both the promise and the danger of a fluid democracy in which the temporary and contingent nature of class renders outward appearances unreliable. The admirable rise of the progenitors of the Chestnut Street "aristocrats" is sullied by the repudiation by their children and grandchildren of the very men on whose fortunes their aristocratic claims rest. Moreover, these beneficiaries of inherited wealth are neither genuine aristocrats nor self-made men but representatives of a frivolous world of fashion. Unable to repose their faith in appearance, the white middle class, rhetorically and literarily, turned to the display of sincerity as the test of the stranger.

31. Harriet E. Wilson, *Our Nig; or, Sketches from the Life of a Free Black* (1859; New York: Vintage, 1983). Hereafter cited parenthetically in the text.

32. For a discussion of Wilson as a reader, see Henry Louis Gates Jr.'s introduction to *Our Nig*, xxxix ff.

33. It is worth noticing that, barring the apparently essential "descent" from country to city, the "plot" and the language of the story of Mag bear a striking resemblance to the purportedly "true" histories of prostitutes offered by George Foster in works like *New York by Gaslight*. While Foster's white prostitutes do not always inhabit the "amalgamated" world of the black-and-tan clubs, their racial status is often compromised.

34. In the context of the preface, as others have noted, the description of Mrs. Bellmont's principles as "southern" seems designed to protect the sensibilities of the northern readers to whom she appeals. As the narrative progresses, however, the distance between "southern principles" and those governing the attitudes and behavior of northern whites diminishes.

35. It is worth considering Wilson's account of the production of "our nig" alongside Walter Johnson's fascinating recent account of the "slave" Alexina Morrison's efforts to prove herself white and therefore free ("The Slave Trade, the White Slave, and the Politics of Racial Determination in the 1850s," *Journal of American History* 87 [June 2000]: 13–38).

36. The slave narrative, with its account of brutality culminating in a liberating moment of rebellion, hovers just behind Wilson's novel.

37. Cynthia J. Davis, "Speaking the Body's Pain: Harriet E. Wilson's *Our Nig*," *African American Review* 27, no. 3 (1993): 392.

38. It is worth noting that the "blacker" Frado becomes, the more her interactions, even with sympathetic whites, echo stock scenes in the novelistic representation of slaves and their masters. Notable among these is the episode in which Frado amuses Jack by refusing to eat from Mrs. Bellmont's plate until it has been licked clean by her dog. Like Mr. Shelby in *Uncle Tom's Cabin*, who throws pennies to Eliza's son Harry when he dances "Jim Crow," Jack throws "a bright, silver half-dollar" at Frado, claiming " 't was worth paying" for his mother's humiliation. A sign of the primarily economic relation in which Frado and the Bellmonts stand, and a sign, in its way, of sympathy as well, this scene nonetheless requires Frado's blackness to be effective.

CHAPTER III

1. Albert S. Bolles, *The Conflict between Labor and Capital* (Philadelphia: Lippincott, 1876), 74. Quoted in Martin J. Burke, *The Conundrum of Class: Public Discourse on the Social Order in America* (Chicago: University of Chicago Press, 1995), 140.

2. The phrase is Burke's from *The Conundrum of Class*. For a discussion of Albert Bolles, William Sylvis, and other "heretics," see chapter 6.

3. I use the term "slavery" advisedly in view of David Roediger's detailed account of the highly fraught use of the tropes of slavery—"wage slavery," "white slavery," "slavery of wages"—by and about white workers prior to Emancipation. See *The Wages of Whiteness* (New York: Verso, 1991), chapter 4. Labor's rhetorical preference for "white slavery," as Roediger has demonstrated, undercuts any suggestion that the critique of the condition of the hireling inevitably contained within it opposition to chattel slavery in the South. That being so, my object is to note two starkly—and broadly—opposed complexes of language, one invoking social harmony, economic mobility, and the freedom of labor, the other insisting on economic fixity, wage "slavery," and the inevitability of violent confrontation.

4. Burke, *The Conundrum of Class*, 141

5. Roediger, *The Wages of Whiteness*, 66.

6. Burke, *The Conundrum of Class*, 144.

7. The ambiguity of Phelps's "millions" and "mills" is nothing if not suggestive, the interchangeability of terms oddly intimating a similar interchangeability of persons.

8. Eric Schocket argues in " 'Discovering Some New Race': Rebecca Harding Davis's 'Life in the Iron Mills' and the Literary Emergence of Working-Class Whiteness" (*PMLA* 115 [2000]: 46–59) that by the 1850s "the language of sentimentalism and its structures of sympathy were so oriented toward issues of race and slavery that anti-industrial social critiques tended . . . to be made in racial terms" (48). Certainly these uses of sentimentalism encouraged the racializing of anti-industrial critiques, but sentimental language is, as I hope to show in this study, "oriented" toward issues of race and class even when its subject is neither race nor slavery nor industrialism. The fact that sentimental writing even or especially in its gender-specific form—in the narrative of the orphan girl—is so deeply engaged with the problem of dependence—and thus, by extension, with class—makes it readily available to writers like Stowe as a vehicle for her antislavery arguments. It is this "prehistory," as it were, to which I hope to draw attention.

9. While I agree with Schocket about the tendency of sentimental critiques of industrial exploitation to exploit a racial logic in which whiteness signifies freedom and blackness slavery (a tendency I earlier outlined in "The Syntax of Class in Elizabeth Stuart Phelps's *The Silent Partner*," in *Rethinking Class*, ed. Michael T. Gilmore and Wai Chee Dimock [New York: Columbia University Press, 1994], 267–85), I want here to highlight the insufficiency of this logic in answering the problem of labor for these authors.

10. David Roediger points out that even when white male workers distanced themselves from the language of slavery, the comparison with chattel slavery was pressed in relation to white women workers and child laborers (*The Wages of Whiteness*, 69–70).

11. Eva, whose mother belongs wholly to the world of profit and self-interest and whose father languishes in poetic indecision, is as effectively orphaned (as I argue in *Prophetic Woman* [Berkley: University of California Press, 1987]), despite Augustine's affection and his wealth, as were her progenitors in domestic fiction.

12. Fanny Fern, *Ruth Hall* (New Brunswick, N.J.: Rutgers University Press, 1986), 3.

13. Harriet Beecher Stowe, *Uncle Tom's Cabin* (1852; Cambridge: Harvard University Press, 1962), 68. Hereafter cited parenthetically in the text as UTC.

14. The democratizing of portraiture—part, surely, of Stowe's point in choosing the daguerreotype as the form for Tom's representation—began with the publicizing of Daguerre's process in 1839. As other critics have suggested, the long exposure time required by daguerreotypy not only produced a deathlike rigidity in the features of the subject but made the dead the perfect subject. Hawthorne exploits this idea in the portraits of the Pyncheons in *The House of the Seven Gables*—as he does the notion that the daguerreotype exposes the truest, most hidden nature of its subject.

15. Rebecca Harding Davis, *Life in the Iron Mills* (1861; Old Westbury, N.Y.: Feminist Press, 1972), 12. Hereafter cited parenthetically in the text as IM.

16. In Dickens's or Gaskell's fictional worlds, where the distinction between masters and men is as sharply drawn as that between master and slave, the evils of industrialization are more readily answerable in the language of sentimentality than they are by Davis or Phelps, for whom the whiteness of the worker should, by all rights, signal his masterless condition. The intersection of class and race so evident in the ideology of free labor, and absent in the English context, forecloses, that is, on the possibility of sentimental representation.

17. Quoted in Eric J. Sundquist, *New Essays on Uncle Tom's Cabin* (New York: Cambridge University Press, 1986), 9.

18. Fanny Fern in *Rose Clark*, quoted in Nina Baym, *Woman's Fiction* (Ithaca: Cornell University Press, 1978), 33. Susan Warner insisted that her 1850 bestseller *The Wide, Wide World* was no "novel" but only a "story." Likewise, Fanny Fern refused to "dignify" *Ruth Hall* by calling it a novel.

19. Harriet Beecher Stowe, *The Key to Uncle Tom's Cabin* (New York: Arno Press, 1969), v.

20. Ibid., vi.

21. "The Tartarus of Maids" deploys erudite, "literary" language from the start: Melville's narrator passes through a "Dantean gateway" into a gorge called the "Devil's Dungeon" where the paper mill is located. As horrified as is Davis's narrator by the exploitation he witnesses there, Melville's narrator has no difficulty in seeing or in recounting what he sees—even when what he sees is his own complicity in the exploitative practices of the mill.

22. See, e.g., Maribel W. Molyneaux, "Sculpture in the Iron Mills: Rebecca Harding Davis's Korl Woman," *Women's Studies* 17 (1990): 157–77; Jean Pfaelzer, "Rebecca Harding Davis: Domesticity, Social Order, and the Industrial Novel," *International Journal of Women's Studies* 4 (May–June 1981): 234–44; Tillie Olsen, "A Biographical Interpretation," in Davis, *Life in the Iron Mills*, 69–174.

23. Quoted in George M. Frederickson, *The Black Image in the White Mind* (New York: Harper, 1971), 106–7.

24. On romantic racialism see ibid., chapter 4.

25. Karen Halttunen, *Confidence Men and Painted Women* (New Haven: Yale University Press, 1982), 83.

26. Uncle Tom is, as Elizabeth Ammons, Jane Tompkins, James Baldwin, and others have argued in various ways and contexts, both infantilized *and* feminized. Likewise, as Jean Pfaelzer has suggested in "Rebecca Harding Davis: Domesticity, Social Order, and the Industrial Novel" (*International Journal of Women's Studies* 4 [1981]: 234–44), Hugh Wolfe—whose sobriquet is "Molly Wolfe" and whose representative is the korl woman—is both a feminized character and a figure for the female artist. In conjunction with my own, this line of argument suggests that one way to lend "plasticity" to the otherwise intractable millworker was to associate him with women, who, like chattel slaves, were understood by sentimental writers to be infinitely malleable subjects.

27. For a discussion of the invocation of the "promise of Dawn" as "ironic posture" see Sharon M. Harris, *Rebecca Harding Davis and American Realism* (Philadelphia: University of Pennsylvania Press, 1991), 56. Unlike Harris, I see the redemption of Deborah by the Quakers as similarly undermined by the narrator's relentless refusal to allow her "dilettante" reader a way out.

28. Halttunen, *Confidence Men and Painted Women*, 192.

29. Jane Tompkins, *Sensational Designs: The Cultural Work of American Fiction, 1790–1860* (New York: Oxford University Press, 1985), 124.

30. Cited in Olsen, "A Biographical Interpretation," 153.

31. Elizabeth Stuart Phelps, "Stories That Stay," *Century Magazine*, November 1910, quoted in Harris, *Rebecca Harding Davis and American Realism*, 308.

32. Stuart M. Blumin, among others, has argued that class was not only an absorbing question in this period but "the most clearly defined social structure in American history," and that "the deepest awareness among Americans of the classes that divided them, emerged in the years following the Civil War." See Blumin, *The Emergence of the Middle Class* (New York: Cambridge University Press, 1989), 258.

33. Elizabeth Stuart Phelps, *The Silent Partner* (1871; Old Westbury, N.Y.: Feminist Press, 1983), 245. Hereafter cited parenthetically in the text as SP.

34. Burke, *The Conundrum of Class*, 136. For Sylvis on the question of the "equal partnership" of labor and capital, see ibid., 140 ff.

35. For discussions of the working-girl melodrama as a popular literary form in this period, see Dorothy S. Pam, "Exploitation, Independence, and Solidarity: The Changing Role of American Working Women as Reflected in the Working-Girl Melodrama, 1870–1910" (Ph.D. diss., New York University, 1980); Mary Noel, *Villains Galore: The Heyday of the Popular Story Weekly* (New York: Macmillan, 1954); Michael Denning, *Mechanic Accents: Dime Novels and Working-Class Culture in America* (New York: Verso, 1987).

36. See, e.g., 48, 54, 189, 294, 295, 300.

37. Elizabeth Stuart Phelps, *Chapters from a Life* (Boston, 1896; reprint, New York: Arno, 1980), 259.

38. Ibid.

39. I have in mind here works like George G. Foster's *New York by Gaslight*, James Dabney McCabe Jr.'s *The Secrets of the Great City*, or Matthew Hale Smith's *Sunshine and Shadow in New York*.

40. Blumin, *Emergence of the Middle Class*, 2.

41. Margaret Oliphant, "American Books," *Blackwood's Magazine*, October 1871, 423.

42. For a discussion of the figure of Catty and the role of disability and the disabled woman, in particular, in mid-nineteenth-century reform fiction, see Rosemarie Garland Thomson, *Extraordinary Bodies: Figuring Physical Disability in American Culture and Literature* (New York: Columbia University Press, 1997), 98 ff.

43. It is worth noting that, in her vulnerability and dependence, the deaf, dumb, and blind Catty occupies the space conventionally inhabited by children—or kittens—in domestic fiction. The maternal impulses that prove womanhood and provide the ground for larger social engagement in that fiction find their place in an analogy that reflects relative social "ability": Perley, that is, "mothers" Sip, and Sip, in turn, "mothers" Catty.

Chapter IV

1. Charles Loring Brace, *The Dangerous Classes of New York and Twenty Years' Work among Them* (New York: Wynkoop & Hallenbeck, 1880; reprint, Montclair, N.J.: Patterson Smith, 1967), 29. Hereafter cited parenthetically in the text.

2. Brace cites both the New York draft riots of 1863 and the Orange riot of 1871 as signs of the danger of the "dangerous classes" (30).

3. The racialized term "street arab" has not, to my knowledge, attracted the attention it would seem to merit in discussions either of race or class.

4. Only twice did Alger devote himself to female protagonists, once in the melodramatic *Helen Ford* (1866) and again in *Tattered Tom* (1871), the story of a street-sweeping boy-girl.

5. Horatio Alger Jr., *Ragged Dick and Mark, the Match Boy* (1867; New York: Macmillan, 1962), 43–44. Hereafter cited parenthetically in the text.

6. Nina Baym, *Novels, Readers, and Reviewers: Responses to Fiction in Antebellum America* (Ithaca: Cornell University Press, 1984), 211. For one kind of account of middle-class unease with representations of urban poverty, see 209–13.

7. On Alger's strenuous efforts to avoid the proletarianizing of his boy protagonists, see Carol Nackenoff, "Of Factories and Failures: Exploring the Invisible Factory Gates of Horatio Alger, Jr.," *Journal of Popular Culture* 25, no. 4 (1992): 63–81.

8. Stansell, *City of Women: Sex and Class in New York, 1789–1860* (Chicago: University of Illinois, 1987). Hereafter cited parenthetically in the text.

9. Deb's purification by the Quakers and Perley's evolution into "womanliness" may be seen as gestures in the direction of reclaiming a narrative of ascent, as attempts to lend the industrial narrative momentum. Given the difficulty of that attempt, it is hardly surprising that the particular means of Deb's redemption are given short shrift by the narrator of *Life in the Iron Mills*: "There is no need," she tells her reader of Deb, "to tire you with the long years of sunshine and fresh

air, and slow, patient Christ-love, needed to make healthy and hopeful this impure body and soul" (63).

10. According to Frank Luther Mott, *Ragged Dick* sold more than 300,000 copies during its first year in print. See *Golden Multitudes: The Story of Best Sellers in the United States* (New York: Macmillan, 1947). This initial success was not maintained despite Alger's remarkable productivity; not until the first decades of the twentieth century did Alger find the wide readership we associate with him. The question of who purchased Alger's novels is a vexed one. It has, however, been persuasively argued that industrial wage earners did not figure prominently among them. See Michael Denning, *Mechanic Accents: Dime Novels and Working-Class Culture in America* (New York: Verso, 1987), 170–71.

11. In 1868, a *Harper's* columnist recalled an earlier day: "The 'boot-black' . . . is a modern invention. A few years ago boot-blacking in New York was done in a very different manner. The boot-blacks were then almost exclusively negro men. They had their workshops and their regular customers, whom they served with clean boots pretty much as the newsboys serve their customers with papers. Every customer was expected to have at least two pairs of boots; the boot-black called at the customer's room early every morning, taking away the dirty and leaving the clean pair. . . . This custom . . . has now become obsolete, and the 'boot-black brigade' has carried all before it." Quoted in Nancy Koppelman, "Icons of the American Dream: Bootblacks and Shoeshine Boys, 1858–1992" (unpublished, by permission of the author).

12. As if his name were not sufficient, Johnny Nolan is supplied with an abusive drunken father to attest to his Irishness. Provided, against his will, with a comfortable place on a farm—presumably through the agency of a charity like the Children's Aid Society—Johnny finds that the solace of plentiful meals and a soft bed does not compensate for loneliness; trading food for friends, he jumps a freight car and returns to New York.

13. Davis, *Life in the Iron Mills*, 37.

14. See Nackenoff, "Of Factories and Failures." Nackenoff observes that there are no factories in any of the cities about which Alger writes. The single and telling exception, as she notes, is "Ben Bruce," serialized in 1892, in which, just as Ben is about to take a job in a leather factory, the factory dam is blown up and the boy saved from industrial labor. Nackenoff reproduces an illustration from *Harper's Weekly* from the 1850s of particular relevance to *Ragged Dick* in which Barnum's American Museum, one of the sights on Dick's tour of New York, is shown and, alongside it, two hat-manufacturing establishments and a building whose sign reads "Billiard Table Factory."

15. For a discussion of the increasing bifurcation of blue- and white-collar work in postbellum urban America, see Stuart M. Blumin, *The Emergence of the Middle Class* (New York: Cambridge University Press, 1989), especially chapter 8. I am indebted to Brian Luskey (unpublished MS) for my understanding of the sexual and moral ambiguity that attended the figure of the midcentury clerk.

16. See, in particular, Madonne M. Miner's "Horatio Alger's *Ragged Dick*: Projection, Denial, and Double-Dealing," *American Imago* 47, nos. 3–4 (1990): 233–48.

17. With an odd disregard of gender, Dick himself characterizes his transformation in this way. "It reminds me," he says, "of Cinderella when she was changed into a fairy princess. I see it one night at Barnum's" (58).

18. For a discussion of the ways homoeroticism plays out in *Ragged Dick*, see Michael Moon, " 'The Gentle Boy from the Dangerous Classes': Pederasty, Domesticity, and Capitalism in Horatio Alger," *Representations* 19 (Summer 1987): 87–110. Alger's expulsion from the Unitarian ministry on charges of pederasty is discussed in Richard Huber, *The American Idea of Success* (New York: , 1971), and in Gary Scharnhorst, *The Lost Life of Horatio Alger, Jr.* (Bloomington: University of Indiana Press, 1985).

19. For a discussion of the types of the "gentle boy" in Alger's novels, see Moon, "Gentle Boy from the Dangerous Classes," 92–93, 98.

20. For a discussion of the adoption of Mark, the match boy, in the novel of that title and of Dick's nine-month's "nest egg" in *Ragged Dick*, see ibid., 99–100.

21. Interestingly, even Micky achieves a modicum of respectability by the third volume of the *Ragged Dick* series. Employed as an errand boy by Dick, himself now a bookkeeper, Micky's prospects are limited (he has "already turned out much better than was expected" [300]), but his respect for Dick and his diligence at work suggest that he will not, at least, fall back into destitution.

22. For a discussion of the twinning of Dick and the thief Jim Travis, see Miner, "Horatio Alger's *Ragged Dick*," 244–45.

23. Alcott's difficulty in completing *Work* is documented in *Louisa May Alcott: Her Life, Letters, and Journals*, ed. Ednah D. Cheney (Boston: Roberts Brothers, 1890).

24. Elizabeth Langland, "Female Stories of Experience: Alcott's *Little Women* in Light of *Work*," in *The Voyage In: Fictions of Female Development*, ed. Elizabeth Abel, Marianne Hirsch, and Elizabeth Langland (Hanover, N.H.: University Press of New England, 1983), 114, 116.

25. Louisa May Alcott, *Work: A Story of Experience* (1873; New York: Schocken, 1977), 442. Hereafter cited parenthetically in the text.

26. The millennial fervor of the ending of *Work* is, of course, framed by Christianity, and more particularly by the socially conscious doctrine Christie discovers and embraces in the congregation of Rev. Powers, a thinly disguised stand-in for Theodore Parker. Supplying the impetus to social action, this doctrine is, I would urge, of less interest theologically than politically. While Christie's emergence as a "mediator" at the end of the novel clearly alludes to the example of her namesake, religion functions in *Work* less as an ideological framework than as a locus for the commitment to social justice.

27. The drift of girls like Christie from New England farm to factory that characterized the 1820s and 1830s, while recalled later in the century in the memoirs of writers like Lucy Larcom, was much diminished by the time of *Work*'s production. Moreover, the plight of "respectable" women who found themselves dependent on their own labor in urban centers like Boston and New York was already a staple of journalism by the 1860s.

28. The nationalities of the "immigrant women" at the intelligence office are not specified, but it is worth noting that the one ethnic group toward which Alcott

is consistently unsympathetic, if not hostile, is the Irish. The "Katy" who precedes Christie in service to the Stuarts is condemned by her as a racist for her unwillingness to share a table with the African American Hepsey (24) and, tellingly, has no objection to the degrading task of bootblacking. On leaving the Stuarts, Christie decides not to continue in service because she knows that she "would never live with Irish mates" (34). In *Work* as in *Little Women* and elsewhere, Alcott's protagonists consistently speak with disdain of the incompetence of Irish "girls."

29. The special position of the "woman" is reiterated in this episode, in which an overturned candle sets Christie's dresses afire when she falls asleep while reading in bed. Frightened and angry, Mrs. Stuart forgets her dignity and reveals her true vulgarity by "scold[ing] like any shrew" (32). Having thus exposed the inferiority of the "lady" to the woman who is her servant, Mrs. Stuart is "inexorable" in her decision to dismiss Christie.

30. It is tempting to understand Christie's wooing of Rachel by way of Caroll Smith-Rosenberg's explication of the conventions of nineteenth-century women's romantic friendships in "The Female World of Love and Ritual: Relations between Women in Nineteenth-Century America," in *Disorderly Conduct* (New York: Knopf, 1985), 53–76. Smith-Rosenberg's analysis has been challenged by historians who take more literally the eroticized language of the documents on which her account depends. Even accepting that account, what is distinctive about Alcott's same-sex couple is that Christie's desire for a permanent home with Rachel presses the boundaries of romantic friendship as Smith-Rosenberg describes it. Between the questions of sexual respectability that attend Christie and Rachel's relationship, the trouble it brings, Christie's contemplation of suicide, and the trade-off of Rachel for her brother, this episode has all the earmarks of a twentieth-century lesbian melodrama.

31. For a discussion of the conventions of the "lesbian novel," see Julie L. Abraham, *Are Girls Necessary?* (New York: Routledge, 1996).

EPILOGUE

1. Rosalyn Baxandall, Linda Gordon, and Susan Reverby, eds., *America's Working Women: A Documentary History—1600 to the Present* (New York: Vintage, 1976), 105–8. Hereafter cited parenthetically in the text.

INDEX